harold pinter

University
of Queensland Press ST. LUCIA

Humanities Press NEW YORK

harold pinter

by alrene sykes

© University of Queensland Press, St. Lucia, Queensland, 1970

National Library of Australia registry number AUS 68–3290
ISBN 0 7022 0576 1

Published in U.S.A. by Humanities Press, New York, 1970
SBN 391–00098–5

Set in Imprint 11/12

Printed and bound by Dai Nippon Printing Co. (International) Ltd.,
Hong Kong

Distributed by International Scholarly Book Services, Inc.
Great Britain–Europe

Designed by Cyrelle

for
my mother and father

acknowledgments

I wish to thank the publishers, Methuen and Co. Ltd. and Grove Press, for permission to quote from the plays *The Birthday Party, The Caretaker, The Dwarfs, The Homecoming,* and *A Slight Ache;* Miss Eunice Hanger and Miss Barbara Vernon, for their helpful suggestions when the book was planned; and finally Mr. Pinter himself, not only for his permission to quote from the plays, but also for his kindness and courtesy in giving me information.

contents

1 the comedies of menace: *the room, the dumb waiter, the birthday party*

One of the most dramatic scenes from the brilliant Joseph Losey film *The Servant* (for which Harold Pinter wrote the script) shows the "servant", a swarthily sinister Dirk Bogarde, moving up a shadowy stairway, chanting "I'm getting warm! You're hiding but you'll be caught. You've got a guilty secret, you've got a guilty secret, but you'll be caught. I'm coming to get you, I'm creeping up on you!" while the "master", played by James Fox as blonde, clean-cut English public school gone slightly to seed, waits shuddering with fright behind a curtain, in a vicious adult version of hide-and-seek. Our pity, horror, and revulsion as the victim cringes in the abasement of his fear are sharpened by awareness that the terror comes only because he allows it to come; that he has in fact invited it. With hardly a struggle, he has handed over to the naturally stronger man, his servant, all the implicit superiority of the master's position, and inevitably he is destroyed.

The scene is only in part Harold Pinter, but it might well have come from one of his plays. If social comment is implied in *The Servant* – the destruction, the death-wish, of the aristocrat – then this is not typical of Pinter, who from the beginning has been either praised or blamed for his apparent indifference to social problems. What is recognizably Pinter, however, is the probing exploration of man's most intimate fears, Pinter's dominant interest not only in the early dramas such as *The Room, The Dumb Waiter,* and *The Birthday Party* (the plays which were so quickly and aptly labelled "comedies of menace" and which seem on the surface to be closest to this scene from *The Servant*), but also in later, less overtly violent dramas. Many of Pinter's characters destroy themselves; and the natural state of a Pinter character is insecurity. This is not of course because he desires or seeks insecurity; the Pinter being is no James Bond. He often puts up a frantic struggle to keep his slipping foothold, he clings to the known, the comfortingly familiar, which may be represented by a room to live in, sheltered from the cold, as in *The Room* and *The Caretaker,* or, for the more sophisticated and "civilized" Teddy of *The Homecoming,* a way of life that will allow him to look down, securely aloof and uninvolved, on the jungle of action around him. It is a lost cause. In spite of his yearnings, the Pinter anti-hero is not allowed to be secure. In the earlier and more melodramatic plays, loss of security leads to physical maiming and even death; in the later ones, where the insecurity seems often to be sexual, the plays tend to end in loss of peace of mind where the love and/or marriage partner is concerned, in *The Homecoming* with the loss of the wife herself, in *The Basement* with the loss of the lover – though this of course is, particularly in the case of *The Basement,* only one facet of Pinter's habitually enigmatic conclusion.

Pinter's three earliest plays, *The Room, The Dumb Waiter,* and *The Birthday Party,* were, in spite of their ambiguities and their affinities with the Absurd, more open than the plays that followed in their onslaught on our fears: they come closest to being superbly effective intellectual thrillers. It was with good reason that Pinter's technique in these early plays was often compared with that of Alfred Hitchcock. Dramatists on all levels have recognized the potential terrors of the situation where a victim waits for a door to open and menace to enter, as for instance when Johnny Boyle in O'Casey's *Juno and the Paycock* cowers in his mother's house and waits for the inevitable retribution of the I.R.A. which he has betrayed; but Pinter's consistent preoccupation with this situation in his earliest plays became almost a trademark. In his first one-act play, *The Room,* Pinter presented his formula for the destruction of security: a room, inhabited by the characters; a door, which opened; and menace, which entered through the door and destroyed the security of the characters. Talking about his method of approach in an early and oft-quoted B.B.C. interview, Pinter himself said:

> Two people in a room – I am dealing a great deal of the time with this image of two people in a room. The curtain goes up on the stage, and I see it as a very potent question: What is going to happen to these people in the room? Is someone going to open the door and come in?

The door opened in *The Room*; it opened again in *The Dumb Waiter*; and it opened for a third time in *The Birthday Party*. It could perhaps be suggested that it has continued to open in every play since, including the recent television drama, *The Basement*; but on the whole it has tended to open more quietly, and the menace to the characters, if still formidable, is less overt.

The repetition of situation in the first three plays was, however, quite blatant, and even Pinter's most sympathetic audiences might have been excused for wondering if he would ever in fact have anything further to say – even though the plays were getting better all the time, and *The Birthday Party* was markedly more substantial than its predecessors. It is still true that Pinter tends to repeat himself, to explore the same areas over and over, from different angles; the saving grace is that he does show new facets, new illuminations, and that he is constantly concerned with technical experiment, exploring the potentials of his medium, be it stage, film, radio, or television screen. With Pinter, the next play is always the unpredictable play, though at the same time one can be reasonably sure that some at least of the landmarks will be familiar. This is true not only of the later plays, but of *The Room, The Dumb Waiter,* and *The Birthday Party.* One could point, for instance, to the variations he rings in his presentation of the all-important room. A room for Pinter is never simply a box in which his characters are encased. It represents security, of course, and somewhere to shelter from the cold; dominance within a room, so that you are in possession of it and what it contains, also confers certain important rights. Pinter wrote a short story (published in the same volume as *The Collection* and *The Lover*) called *The Examination,* which concerns two men, the narrator of the story and another called Kullus, and the changes of dominance within the room. In the beginning, the room belongs to the narrator—as he says: "Yet I was naturally dominant, by virtue of my owning the room", and he keeps the windows and curtains open, according to his taste. He remembers a time, however, when the room was Kullus's room, and Kullus dictated the arrangement of window and curtain, "seldom to my taste or my comfort". The "plot" of the story traces how the narrator, interrogating Kullus, gradually loses his ascendancy, and Kullus takes command, removes the blackboard, and closes the curtains. The narrator does not object, for, as he says in the closing lines of the story, "we were now in Kullus's room". This sense of possessiveness towards a room, and awareness of the rights that ownership of a room confers, run through several of Pinter's plays, including *A Slight Ache* and of course *The Caretaker*; and it is visually most interestingly used in the television play, *The Basement,* where the appearance of the room reflects the changing situation and the reversals of dominance between the characters – a rather more complex version of Kullus's and the narrator's manoeuvrings with curtains, window, blackboard, and table. As Law's apartment at the beginning of the play, the room is commonplace, over-furnished, comfortable. When Stott takes command, one of the first signs of the assertion of his rights is that he takes down the pictures, and Law accepts his condemnation of them; the room becomes stark, bare, modern Swedish. Next it becomes baroque; Law plays his flute, and the two men engage in ritual duels against a lush background of carvings, gilt, leaded windows. At the very end, as the play comes round full circle, as it begins once more with the opening situation and opening dialogue, but with Law now outside in the rain and Stott reading comfortably inside, the room has once more assumed its early pleasantly banal appearance.

This kind of rapid change of set belongs essentially to the television medium rather than the stage, and to a play quite different in character to any of Pinter's three early dramas; in them, he attempts nothing so extreme with his settings. The rooms of *The Room, The Birthday Party,* and *The Dumb Waiter* are probably sufficiently alike to be found in the same street. They belong to what used to be called working-class people: Bert of *The Room* drives a van, Petey in *The Birthday Party* is a deckchair attendant; it is perhaps more difficult to gauge the exact social status of the hired gunmen, Gus and Ben, of *The Dumb Waiter,* belonging as they do to a rather exotic profession. Stage directions seem to suggest simple and rather old-fashioned furniture for these rooms, and the room of *The Birthday Party* (the living room of a seaside boarding house which never seems to have any boarders, except the victim, Stanley) is presumably not only shabby but dirty. Stanley himself seems to be not over-fussy about cleanliness and baths and shaving, but even he comments irritably to Meg, the landlady:

Look, why don't you get this place cleared up! It's a pigsty.

However, one would expect that Pinter, who in spite of his notorious speech repetitions is actually one of the most economical of playwrights, would put his settings to work; and this of course he does, each one in a slightly different way.

The importance of the room, as a shelter and as a fiercely defended possession, is most forcibly stressed in the first play, *The Room* – as the title might suggest. When the curtain rises, Rose, a motherly, talkative being of about sixty is getting breakfast for her husband Bert, one of Pinter's taciturn males who throughout the scene says not a single word. Rose however chatters on, largely about the room, and how warm it is compared with the cold and darkness outside, and how much better than the basement it is. As she says, it is a place where "you know where you are. When it's cold, for instance", and "you can come home, you're all right. And I'm here. You stand a chance." It is a room not to be polluted by strangers and invaders. Rose tells the blind negro Riley, who has waited all weekend in the basement to speak to her:

My luck. I get these creeps come in, smelling up my room.

But the security of the room exists only in Rose's mind. Flickering doubts about it arise – Did Mr. Kidd (who may or may not be the landlord) once live in it? Has he seen the armchair and the rocking chair before? Then a young couple wanting to rent a room, a Mr. and Mrs. Sands, knock on the door and tell Rose that the man in the basement said that number seven was vacant. Rose says slowly:

That's this room.

Where now is the security represented by her ownership of the room? Anything might happen, and does, with the melodramatic entry of the blind negro who says to her:

Come home, Sal.

Towards the end of the play, the banality of the surroundings makes sharp contrast with the melodramatic, even bizarre, happenings within the room; perhaps not only contrast but a suggestion for the audience that "this could happen to you". This contrast is exploited again in *The Dumb Waiter* and *The Birthday Party*. In *The Dumb Waiter,* Gus and Ben certainly have no pride of possession in their surroundings – the room this time is simply an unfamiliar basement room where they, as professional killers, are waiting to do a job – but a great deal is made of the ordinariness, the homely familiarity of the room. Ben and Gus discuss the furnishings, making sure that we, the audience, do not overlook them: the photograph of the first eleven on the wall, the sheets (which pong), and the kettle and the gas stove, the black and white striped china. It is not a room to be over-confident about, however. Even the lavatory does not flush until some minutes after the chain is pulled; matches appear mysteriously under the door; and down through the wall comes rattling a dumb waiter, bringing weird and increasingly exotic orders for food which drive Ben and Gus into a frenzy of anxiety and futile activity. If one needs help in accepting the bizarre, perhaps the fact that the room is a basement, somehow more cut off from the world than a room above ground level, helps one to believe that anything could happen here. (Pinter's latest television play, one of his most exotic, takes place largely in the basement from which it is named – *The Basement.*) Finally, the structure of the room is used towards the shock ending of the play. The basement has no windows, but it has two doors, left and right. No one uses the door right, the stage directions say it leads to a passage; but throughout the play Gus is constantly disappearing through the door left, which apparently leads to the kitchen and lavatory. It is through the door right that their victim will appear. At the end of the play, Gus as usual goes out through door left to the kitchen, and Ben, alone on stage, receives his final orders through the speaking tube. He calls Gus, the lavatory flushes off left as usual (a typical Pinter combination of low comedy at the moment of terror?), and for the first time the door *right* opens. In stumbles Gus, "stripped of his jacket, waistcoat, tie, holster and revolver", and in silence the two men stare at each other. The one certainty is that Gus is the victim; but crashing doubts ask "why?" and what happened outside the door that he should appear thus?

In *The Birthday Party,* the room (the living room of a seaside boarding-house) presumably represents security to Stanley, the boarder, since he seems to be in hiding, or at least never goes out. "Why don't you ever go out?" asks Lulu, the more-than-friendly girl next door. The person who is proud and possessive towards the room in this case is Meg, the landlady, for whom the house is a very good boarding-house and "on the list", though it does seem highly likely that Stanley has in fact been her only guest. But one is less aware in *The Birthday Party* of the room as a room; it lacks the slightly claustrophobic feeling of the earlier rooms, patently it is only one of several in the house inhabited by the characters. There is still the same feeling of familiarity, ordinariness, and credibility about the setting, in contrast to the strange things that happen against it; but this time it comes from people, rather than objects. In terms of plot, Meg and her husband Petey play quite a minor role, but they are on stage as the curtain rises, thoroughly credible, as Petey reads and Meg chatters (very much in the manner of the opening of *The Room*), and they discuss items from the social columns of the paper, such as Lady Mary Splatt's baby, while Petey eats his cornflakes and fried bread. At the end of the play, after the disastrous non-birthday party which has reduced Stanley to a mindless wreck, Meg is still concerned with breakfast and cornflakes; and they remain behind in their room, as Stanley is carried off into the unknown, their lives, it would seem, to continue very much as before.

For all the subtlety with which he may exploit them, Pinter's rooms are still basically only a background to what happens to the people in them: that is, destruction at the hands of menace. In the theatre, Pinter's menace is not less arresting because it is not precisely defined: Pinter works on the surely indisputable assumption that all human beings are capable of fear, that most of us have at some time feared the unknown, and that we are as capable of responding to the terrors of his menace without understanding exactly what it is about as we are of responding to the hopelessness of Vladimir and Estragon in *Waiting for Godot* without understanding precisely what Beckett's play is about either. It is quite possible that Pinter's

menace is the more frightening simply because we can read into
it our own particular bogeymen. Away from the theatre, we will
probably start asking some questions. What is Pinter's menace –
can the essence of it be detected? Why does it come? Is it completely irrational, representing the disastrous event, unforeseen
and unforeseeable, that may come at any time in any life? Is it a
projection of subconscious fears? Is it a punishment, perhaps
even a specific punishment for a specific guilt?

Geographically, Pinter's menace might be said to lie halfway
between that of Kafka (in *The Trial* and *The Castle*) and that of
Max Frisch (in *The Fire Raisers*). In a sense, Pinter is closer to
Kafka, and the hidden, inner world of guilt and fear, than to
Frisch, who presents the concrete results of man's failure as a
social being, with a suggestion of didacticism and social comment
by the author; but he is like Frisch in focussing attention on
the visible agents of menace, rather than on some obscure higher
source of menace lying behind them. In Kafka, the unseen
controllers of trial and castle have a nightmare pervasiveness,
beside which their agents seem almost puny; in Pinter, though
we are aware of the likelihood of some unseen higher power or
organization behind the agents of menace, it remains shadowy,
and the terror comes from the agents themselves.

Pinter's agents of menace have human faces. The menace
of *The Room* is Riley, the blind negro, who comes to tell
Rose:

> Your father wants you to come home.

In *The Dumb Waiter*, it is the victim's fellow-inhabitant of the
room, his professional partner, as it were, who is transformed into
executioner. In *The Birthday Party*, menace appears in the shape
of two gentlemen, the apparently genial Jew, Goldberg, and the
dour Irishman, McCann, who come to stay in Meg's boarding
house, and who systematically reduce Stanley to speechless idiocy
with a terrifying and at first seemingly illogical interrogation and
a game of blind man's buff that nearly ends in murder, before
carrying him off to further untold horrors and presumably death.
We are aware that a rational, everyday explanation of these beings
and their actions might be possible, but it is not given. The exact
nature of the menace remains emphatically unknown. The essence
of the Pinter world, as Martin Esslin has suggested, is that "we

are surrounded by the unknown".[1] Pinter is reluctant to provide
a dossier on anyone, particularly in the early plays, and any
explanations or facts about his creatures of menace normally add
to our confusion, for instance the self-contradictory autobiographies expansively delivered by Goldberg in *The Birthday Party*.
To add to the mystery of these agents, some are given a hint of
possible supernatural powers, or at least prescience. Riley tells
Mr. and Mrs. Sands with authority that room number seven (the
room inhabited by Rose and Bert) will be vacant. Goldberg does
not need to see the house-number to find Meg's and Petey's
house, and when McCann asks him how he knows this is the
right house –

I didn't see a number on the gate

– he and Goldberg are already comfortably ensconced in the
living room. With superb authority, Goldberg replies simply:

I wasn't looking for a number.

(Or had he simply been down earlier to investigate?) Even before
he has met Lulu, Goldberg asked Stanley:

Why do you treat the young lady like a leper?

A rational explanation? Of course, one is possible; but one tends
instead to accept the psychic powers of the Pinter menace. Ben is
admittedly much more prosaic, as he demonstrates that menace
can in fact be executed through one's fellow inhabitant of the
room, and the mystification of *The Dumb Waiter* is expressed
chiefly through the bizarre dumb waiter itself.

However, for all their terror and mystery, the beings we see
are in fact agents of some invisible removed power, like Kafka's,
the difference being, as already suggested, that Pinter does not
build up this unseen power so that it overshadows the visible
agents; but obviously our awareness of its hovering presence
increases their stature. Riley says he comes from Rose's father –

Your father wants you to come home.

Ben takes orders from someone; he stands at attention by the
speaking tube down which apparently come directions to dispose

---

1. *The Theatre of the Absurd* (London: Eyre and Spottiswoode, 1962), p. 212.

of Gus, by their normal methods. We suspect that the invisible source of these orders may be Wilson, Gus and Ben's boss, whose name is several times in the play uneasily mentioned by Gus. Goldberg and McCann insist, when Petey wants them to leave him to look after the shattered Stanley, that they are taking Stanley to Monty for "special treatment"; the special treatment has a sinister ambiguity, and again there is the suggestion that Monty is a higher authority. Pinter tells us very little about these "higher authorities". Rose's father and Monty are mentioned only briefly (we know of their existence but nothing else about them), and though Gus does frequently speak of Wilson, he says little more than that he finds him hard to talk to, and that he "doesn't seem to bother about our comfort these days". Perhaps Rose's father, Wilson, and Monty are themselves merely agents of some higher and more remote power, and the chain of authority goes on and on, like Vladimir's song, in *Waiting for Godot,* about the dog who came into the kitchen and stole a piece of bread.

It seems fitting that mere agents should not themselves be invulnerable. As J.R. Taylor suggested:

> *The Dumb Waiter* assures us, hired killers are just men like anyone else; they only obey orders, and while menacing others they themselves can also be menaced.[2]

One could go further and add that in Pinter's plays the agents of menace are always vulnerable, not only in *The Dumb Waiter.* There could be no arguing that Riley is vulnerable, since he is apparently killed when Bert knocks him down at the end of the play. There is even a scene, a strange and quite moving scene, in *The Birthday Party,* which may suggest that Goldberg and McCann in spite of their impressive front are also vulnerable, though not in this play broken.[3] In this scene they, and particularly McCann, show signs of being themselves affected by the torment they have inflicted on Stanley.

> MCCANN (*turning to look at* GOLDBERG, *grimly*). I'm not going up there again.
> GOLDBERG. Why not?
> MCCANN. I'm not going up there again.

---

2. *Anger and After* (London: Methuen, 1962), p. 239.
3. *The Birthday Party and Other Plays* (London: Methuen, 1960), pp. 75–83.

GOLDBERG. What's going on now?
MCCANN (*moving down*). He's quiet now. He stopped all that. . . talking a while ago.

Even Goldberg admits a fatigue uncommon to him. As the scene proceeds, Goldberg half kills McCann when McCann tentatively and experimentally calls him "Simey"; then there follows a monologue from Goldberg, broken, laden with meaningless clichés, the despairing empty utterances of a hollow man:

GOLDBERG. . . . That's why I've reached my position, McCann. Because I've always been as fit as a fiddle. All my life I've said the same. Play up, play up, and play the game. Honour thy father and thy mother. All along the line. Follow the line, the line, McCann, and you can't go wrong. What do you think, I'm a self-made man? No! I sat where I was told to sit. I kept my eye on the ball. School? Don't talk to me about school. Top in all subjects. And for why? Because I'm telling you, I'm telling you, follow my line? Follow my mental? Learn by heart. Never write down a thing. No. And don't go too near the water. And you'll find – that what I say is true.
Because I believe that the world. . . (*Vacant.*). . . .
Because I believe that the world. . . (*Desperate.*). . . .
BECAUSE I BELIEVE THAT THE WORLD. . . (*Lost.*). . . .

The scene continues in this grotesque, comic-pathetic strain, for the moment at least quite changing our vision of Goldberg and McCann.

Although Pinter firmly denies that he uses symbolism in his plays, it is very difficult, in our symbol-conscious age, to avoid reading symbolism into them. In discussions of Pinter's menace, some critics have put up persuasive arguments that his menace may be more precisely identified; it has been suggested for instance that it represents such forces as religion, or society, which destroy contemporary man, crushing his individuality and identity. But for the most part the ambiguity of the menace has been stressed, the fact that it is unknown, mysterious; and there is often the added implication that the reason for its coming is inexplicable, even irrational.

To say that the coming of the menace is irrational, wholly governed by chance, is surely a distortion of it. Certainly the agent of menace always seems to know why he has come, and he has always apparently a specific purpose, specific orders to carry out;

even more importantly, the victim himself seems to understand what is afoot, and invariably recognizes his destroyer, or the fact that someone is going to destroy him. His recognition is never simply a vague acceptance of guilt, in the sense of the famous surmise that if you send anyone at all a message that "all is discovered" he or she will flee the country. Pinter's characters in these early plays show every sign of guilty consciences; and there is an ever increasing tendency, from play to play, to give the audience at least a strong hint of the nature of the victim's guilt, what might have brought the menace down upon his head–though certainly this is never brought right out into the open or expressed in cut and dried terms.

Riley in *The Room* is at once Pinter's vaguest and most specific presentation of menace. For once the agent of menace says immediately and openly why he has come. He tells Rose:

Your father wants you to come home.

and Rose responds instantly, with apparently full comprehension of what he means. Up to this point, she has been voluble and vindictive towards him, talking almost non-stop at the blind man, but at these words she pauses, and her aggressiveness seems to collapse as she says:

Stop it. I can't take it. What do you want? What do you want?

She seems even further shaken when strangely he calls her by the name "Sal". Then she touches him–according to the stage directions

She touches his eyes, the back of his head and his temples with her hands

– Rose who recently had told him:

My luck. I get these creeps come in, smelling up my room.

Rose clearly knows what is afoot, but the exact reverse is true for the audience. For them, the message, "Come home", opens up chasms of ignorance; not only is her future very much in doubt, but we are made forcefully aware how little we know about this ordinary elderly woman, her past, or that of her husband Bert. What does Riley mean to her? Why has he come?

Riley has often been found the least satisfactory and most melodramatic of Pinter's embodiments of menace, hardly surprisingly as *The Room* is his apprentice play. Suggestions that he represents death do not seem quite adequate; if Riley is death, why is Bert able to kill him? Why does his blindness pass to Rose? Probably we are not intended to "interpret" Riley; he may well be merely something unpleasant from the outer darkness. Nevertheless, the temptation to try to explain him is irresistible. It is at least possible that *The Room* is the closest Pinter has come to social criticism. Each in his own way, Bert and Rose represent an attitude of "I'm all right, Jack". Rose's attitude to her room is an intensely possessive one; she is confident of its superiority over the basement and upstairs, and it is a place where she does not have to bother about others.

> We're quiet, we're all right. You're happy up here. It's not far up either, when you come in from the outside. And you're not bothered. And nobody bothers us.

Bert's attitude is different, but still related to that of Rose. He does not bother to speak, to communicate, either to Rose or to Mr. Kidd, though they speak to him, till he is stirred to violent emotion by finding Rose touching the face of the blind negro. If the scene were part of a naturalistic drama, faithfully mirroring life, we would probably not hesitate over the cause of his emotion: a perfectly understandable anger and possessive jealousy over Rose, akin to Rose's possessiveness towards the room. Like Rose, Bert responds to a threat to his possession by becoming aggressive; where Rose became shrewish, he takes the more direct action of knocking the negro down. When he does speak, he does not actually mention the negro, but what he says is an expression of "I'm all right, Jack". His words reveal a power-lust, coming out in the not uncommon form of car-driver's mania, as he describes how he drove his van home ("they got it very icy out"):

> There was no cars. One there was. He wouldn't move. He wouldn't move. I bumped him. I got my road. I had all my own way. There again and back. They shoved out of it. I kept on the straight. There was no mixing it. Not with her. She was good. She went with me. . .

Riley's demand that Rose "come home" might perhaps be a command that she be less isolated; it might imply involvement with a "family", the wider circle of humanity that she is seeking to avoid. In the same way, Riley's presence would represent some kind of threat to Bert's unshared possession of his wife. It is not likely that in making Riley a blind negro Pinter was seeking to draw attention to the problems of the coloured races; but the rather exotic mixture of an Irish name and a black face makes Riley an ideal representative of the "foreign", so often regarded with suspicion and fear by Pinter characters. Bert seeks to dispose of the intruder in his kingdom the only way he knows, by violence. The emissary who has come to summon Rose to the outside world is dead; and Rose has taken on his blindness. The moral, if such an unlikely animal could be said to exist in a Pinter play, might be that "no man is an island", however much he may desire it; and of course, man's "deliberate evasion of communication"[4] when possible, as distinct from his inability to communicate, was to prove one of Pinter's constant themes.

Is it then implied that the advent of menace is actually a punishment, a moral judgment, on wrongdoing? One cannot go so far as this, either in *The Room* or the later plays, *The Dumb Waiter* and *The Birthday Party*. What we do find, in all three, is a kind of suitability about the fate of the victim. Rose, who has consistently refused to communicate with the outside world, is struck blind. It is fitting that Gus, a professional killer, should meet his fate at the hands of a fellow-professional. Stanley may have been a pianist (he has certainly dreamed of being one), and playing the piano is one way of expressing oneself. At the end of *The Birthday Party* the only sounds of self-expression he can make are "Uh-gug. . . uh-gug. . .eeehhh-gag (*on the breath.*) Caaahh. . .caahh. . ." It may be significant that he does not speak after his glasses are broken. Suitability, however, does not necessarily imply poetic justice, although the suitability of the victim's fate does reinforce the impression that some kind of cause-and-effect is at work. Pinter makes no moral judgment on people like Rose who want to remain securely "keeping to themselves" in the sanctuary of the room; he merely demonstrates that it is not always possible.

Why does Gus become a victim in *The Dumb Waiter*? As in *The Room,* the visitation of menace does not seem to be simply irrational, nor is it on the other hand fully explained. Like Rose, Gus (who also seems to sense danger before the audience is fully aware of his need for apprehension) appears to respond to his

---

4. "Pinter Between the Lines", *Sunday Times,* 4 March 1962, p. 25.

fate with recognition, but Gus's recognition has a stronger aura of guilt about it than the one sensed in Rose. He is not necessarily guiltier than Rose, but seems more conscious of guilt, and unlike Rose actually spells out for the audience the reasons why he feels himself to be in danger. This does not mean of course that we can take his word for it; he may not be right. The play itself suggests reasons, beyond the ones apparently accepted by Gus, why he is to be destroyed; but, again, we cannot even be sure of these.

If one could simply take Gus's word, it would be easy enough to "explain" what is happening. Gus thinks, or rather seems to think – one does not lightly take responsibility for expounding the mental processes of a Pinter character – that he is suffering because he is inefficient. The first suggestion of his possible inefficiency comes from the man who is to be his executioner, Ben.

When the play opens, Gus is not yet apprehensive about himself, but he is hardly in a suitably devoted frame of mind about his job. His restlessness is conveyed in carefully cumulative sentences.

> I didn't have a very restful sleep today, did you?
> It's not much of a bed. I could have done with another blanket too.
> ....
> I like to get a look at the scenery. You never get a chance in this job.
> ....
> Don't you ever get a bit fed up?
> ....
> He doesn't bother much about our comfort these days.
> ....
> He's not even laying on any gas now either.

Worse still, Gus has even begun to doubt the nature of his profession, or so it would seem from his ruminations on the mess when they shot the girl, and the looser texture of women. As the dumb waiter rattles up and down, Gus continues to ask questions, about the present situation, who owns the café now, and "What's going on here?", while the more amenable Ben tries to silence his questionings and doubts. Finally Ben openly challenges Gus's efficiency.

> BEN. . . . You're getting lazy, you know that? You don't want to get slack on your job.
> GUS. Who me?

BEN. Slack, mate, slack.
GUS. Who me? Slack?
BEN. Have you checked your gun? You haven't even checked your
gun. It looks disgraceful, anyway. Why don't you ever polish it?

The possibility that he is inefficient registers with Gus, though he does not comment immediately. He begins to worry at this idea of reliability, and in a very human fashion seeks to share the danger with Ben, though clearly it is his own reliability he is concerned about:

I was thinking the other day, Ben. We're reliable, aren't we?

Significantly, it is at this point that Gus shows his first sign of physical deterioration, which is to increase as the play progresses, and he tells Ben:

I'm feeling a bit off. I've got a splitting headache.

However, even his recognition of his own possible inadequacy does not stop Gus from questioning the actions of "him", in contrast to Ben's consistent deference.

What about us?. . . I'm thirsty too. I'm starving. And he wants a cup of tea. That beats the band, that does.

Gus's hysteria and his questions mount in intensity, culminating in a violent outburst, again centred on "our" reliability:

What's he doing it for? We've been through our tests, haven't we? We got right through our tests, years ago, didn't we? We took them together, don't you remember, didn't we? We've proved ourselves before now, haven't we? We've always done our job. What's he doing all this for? What's the idea? What's he playing these games for?

As the dumb waiter rattles down with a last order for scampi, Gus shouts up the tube:

WE'VE GOT NOTHING LEFT! NOTHING! DO YOU UNDERSTAND?

Ben pushes him away and says savagely:

That's enough! I'm warning you!

After this, Gus collapses. He hardly speaks till his final (and silent) entrance, drooping, stripped of jacket and revolver.

Perhaps Gus has become inefficient; anyone who is as half-hearted about his career as Gus seems to be does normally become a little sloppy about it. The suggestion in Gus of the discontented bank clerk, who in spite of his distaste for the job is shocked to find himself fired for inefficiency, gives the play an overall ridiculousness, paralleled on a minor scale by such details as Ben's preoccupation with his woodwork –

> I've got my woodwork. I've got my model boats. Have you ever seen me idle? I'm never idle. I know how to occupy my time, to its best advantage

– and in fact by the constant juxtaposition in the play of the brutal, the bizarre, and the homely and familiar.

But is inefficiency the only reason why Gus must be disposed of? It is also made very clear that Gus is the one who asks questions, who does not accept authority and the established order of things; and his attitude is in marked contrast to the unquestioning deference of Ben, who survives and remains the agent of the unseen powers. This habit of questioning obviously could be a reason why authority should seek to get rid of Gus, and perhaps a more cogent reason than his inefficiency. Such an interpretation, the death of Gus as Questioner, could have numberless reverberations, particularly social and political ones, adding to the dimensions of the play. As usual with Pinter, what we read into the lines depends finally on our own imaginations and experience. It is not clearly stated that Gus is destroyed for asking questions; we are given hints, which we may take or reject as we please.

If Pinter's tendency to suggest underlying cause and effect, and acceptance of guilt, increased from *The Room* to *The Dumb Waiter*, it is even more visible in *The Birthday Party*. Goldberg and McCann have come for a specific purpose, to do a "job" which they discuss at some length. We quickly pick up some idea of the general nature of the job, perhaps when Goldberg asks McCann why he is so nervous, and suggests:

> Everywhere you go these days it's like a funeral

– to which McCann mournfully agrees:

> That's true.

On the other hand, from the moment Stanley hears of the "two gentlemen" who are coming to stay in Meg's house, he acts exactly like a frightened, guilty man who knows that retribution is at hand. He tries to avert the danger by insisting that it cannot happen, that the two gentlemen "won't come", says that "it's a false alarm". In familiar fashion he takes out his fears on someone weaker than himself, Meg, made vulnerable by her affection for him; he asks her:

Have you heard the latest?

and proceeds to tell her about "them", who are coming in a van, with a wheelbarrow in it, a big wheelbarrow –

and when the van stops they wheel it out, and they wheel it up the garden path, and then they knock at the front door. . . They're looking for someone. A certain person.

Meg is satisfyingly terrified. Stanley accepts fatalistically the fact that there can be no escape; and his acceptance heightens our respect for the as yet unseen powers. Before Goldberg and McCann actually arrive, when they are the still the two unidentified gentlemen who are coming to stay, Stanley asks Lulu if she would like to go away with him; she asks where, and Stanley slumps once more into despondency:

Nowhere. There's nowhere to go. So we could just go. It wouldn't matter.

After Goldberg and McCann have arrived, but before Stanley has actually seen them, Meg manages to remember Goldberg's name and repeat it to Stanley. Stanley responds with what seems to be recognition; he does not speak but "slowly sits". The despair he cannot or will not put into words finds vivid theatrical expression, however, as he begins to beat on the child's drum Meg has given him for his birthday, *"his face and the drumbeat now savage and possessed"*.

The first minutes of the meeting between Stanley and McCann sounds like a straightforward drama of retribution in the Irish troubles, of punishment for treachery to the cause – the kind of play that Pinter must surely have many times encountered in his tours of Ireland and the provinces as an actor. At this first meeting, McCann begins whistling "The Mountains of Mourne", and is immediately joined in chorus by Stanley. Stanley tries to persuade McCann that there has been a mistake in identity (though his identity has not been questioned):

> To look at me, I bet you wouldn't think I'd led such a quiet life. The lines on my face, eh? It's the drink. Been drinking a bit down here. But what I mean is... you know how it is... away from your own... all wrong, of course... I'll be all right when I get back... but what I mean is, the way some people look at me you'd think I was a different person.

McCann is impervious to hints, so Stanley tries again. In spite of the fact that "all those years I lived in Basingstoke I never stepped outside the door", it appears that he knows Ireland very well:

> I love that country and I admire and trust its people. I trust them. They respect the truth and they have a wonderful sense of humour. I think their policemen are wonderful.

As the scene unwinds, one cannot help feeling that the sentiments, if not the language, could belong to a cowering O'Casey hero.

The play proceeds in an almost impeccably naturalistic manner until the first "interrogation" of Stanley, which happens to be preceded, if not brought on, by Stanley's whistling "The Mountains of Mourne". The scene begins with a contest of wills between Stanley, Goldberg, and McCann, as to whether Stanley will or will not sit down. Naturally Stanley loses; he is forced to sit, he tries to appear as off-hand and casual as possible about giving in, and for a few moments whistles while they watch him in silence. Goldberg asks:

> Webber, what were you doing yesterday?

And thus commences the most terrifying episode in the play, as Goldberg and McCann, in perfect accord, hurl accusations and questions at Stanley, while Stanley disintegrates before our eyes in abject terror and bewilderment.

The interrogation is by no means as wild, illogical, and meaningless as it might first appear. (An analogy might be suggested on this point at least with Lucky's speech in *Waiting for Godot*.) McCann, not surprisingly, stresses Ireland and betrayal, with special reference to an "organization" which one might well presume to be the I.R.A.:

Why did you leave the organization?

That's a Black and Tan fact.

You betrayed the organization.

What about Ireland?

What about the blessed Oliver Plunkett?

What about Drogheda?

His reference to "the Albigensenist heresy" moves out of Ireland, but remains in the general area of treason and heresy, in a usefully ambiguous reference. Goldberg is more general in his questions and accusations, and more concerned with extracting from Stanley admissions of what he has been doing in the past. He makes repeated references to cleanliness, the date of Stanley's last bath, whether he took Enos or Andrews fruit salts, when he last washed a cup, and "You verminate the sheet of your birth". Sometimes the interrogation seems to proceed purely by association of ideas; for instance, "Joe Soap" leads to "You stink of sin", thence to the association with religion in the "external force, responsible for you, suffering for you", and from there to echoes of the disputations of Aquinas on the necessity and possibility of a divine being, given a ridiculous air by the substitution of a number, 846 (which seems to have no special significance), for the divine being. It is possible that the "external force" idea is picked up again later in the "Why did the chicken cross the road?" passage, with the hint of free will and predestination. There is surely a joke intended as McCann says:

You betrayed our land

and Jewish Goldberg tops it with:

You betrayed our breed.

Certainly audiences laugh at this point.

The total effect is wild, whirling, precisely and humiliatingly personal, and at the same time many-faceted, probing multifarious areas of Stanley's being. On the whole, the majority of the accusations and questions relate to treachery and defilement. Not all; the occasional seemingly illogical indictment "You stuff

yourself with dry toast" increases the terror of the "trial" in that
it leaves us as well as Stanley at sea and groping; but beyond these,
most of the accusations do suggest the kindred corruptions of
treachery and defilement. The scene rings with reverberations
of guilt and betrayal. It appears that Stanley has been guilty of
deceit of some kind, though one could hardly pinpoint it to a
specific betrayal of the I.R.A. It would seem rather that *The
Birthday Party* is an image of insecurity, this time focussed on the
situation of a man who has betrayed someone or something, and
is afraid of the consequences.

A last question one might feel inclined to ask about the Pinter
menace: is there any special reason why the menace that invades
the Pinter room should come at this time and no other? Does
any specific act set the wheels in motion, now and not later?
This does not in fact seem to be the case. Goldberg says in *The
Birthday Party*:

> If we hadn't come today we'd have come tomorrow.

There seems to be no hurry; but the menace is there, and it will
come. Even for the audience, it is not completely unexpected.
Partly we are warned by the tension and apprehension of the
characters: Rose turning shrew; Stanley's vindictiveness towards
Meg; Gus and Ben nearly coming to blows over word usage,
whether one should say "light the kettle" or "light the gas".
In *The Room* we are disturbed by flickering uncertainties, uncertainties about the room, the vacancy of number seven, and even
the uncertain autobiographies of Mr. Kidd, his memories of his
mother –

> I wouldn't be surprised to learn that she was a Jewess. She didn't
> have many babies.

— his sister, where he lives. In *The Dumb Waiter,* the tone is
set for ultimate violence at the very beginning of the play, according to Pinter's usual pattern of pregnant opening lines. It is
comic-grotesque violence, the sick humour of the news items read
aloud by Ben from the newspaper about the man of eighty-seven
who crawled under a stationary lorry and was run over when it
started, and the child of eight who killed a cat:

> BEN. A man of eighty-seven crawling under a lorry!
> GUS. It's unbelievable.

BEN. It's down here in black and white.
GUS. Incredible.

Then the room is invaded by the mysterious and the unknown.
At first the invasions from without are for the audience amusing
rather than alarming; there is nothing specially sinister about the
envelope containing twelve matches which suddenly appears,
pushed under the door by an unknown hand, or even the dumb
waiter, which is almost a living character as it rattles up and down
with its demands, beginning humbly enough with:

> Two braised steak and chips. Two sago puddings. Two teas
> without sugar.

and working up to the more exotic

> One Bamboo Shoots, Water Chestnuts and Chicken. One Char
> Siu and Beansprouts.

At this stage, the dumb waiter is the pivot of some wildly funny
farce. The mood of the play changes as it becomes critical:

> The Eccles cake was stale... The chocolate was melted... The
> milk was sour... The biscuits were mouldy...

and at last demands a cup of tea, a request which becomes less
innocuous when we remember the cup of tea which seems normally to accompany a job for Ben and Gus.

The preliminaries for violence in *The Birthday Party* are briefer
and more direct; we take our clues from Stanley's apprehension
and the early strong hints from Goldberg and McCann about the
funereal nature of their job. The pattern on which *The Birthday
Party* is built is quite different to that of *The Room* and *The
Dumb Waiter*. In both *The Room* and *The Dumb Waiter,* the
greater part of the play is given to the steadily deepening apprehension of the victim, and the final annihilating blow is reserved
for its last moments; in *The Birthday Party,* however, Stanley
is already crushed at the end of the second act, and he makes only
a brief inarticulate appearance in Act III. The third act is largely
concerned with the effect of his fate on other people – one reason
why *The Birthday Party* is a more complex and wider-reaching
play than its predecessors. In this play Pinter introduces into the
fabric of invasion-of-menace the bystanders, the people who have

seen a fellow human being destroyed and lifted no hand to save him, and who face a future of living with this knowledge.

Particularly on the grounds of these three early plays, *The Room, The Dumb Waiter,* and *The Birthday Party,* Harold Pinter has been claimed more than once to be one of the very few British representatives of the drama of the Absurd; and analogies have been drawn again and again between Pinter and Samuel Beckett. At the time when Pinter's career as a playwright was beginning, Samuel Beckett was just becoming fashionable among the initiated in England. *Waiting for Godot* had its first famous production at the Babylone in Paris in 1952; English translations were published in New York in 1954, and in London in 1956. The play appeared on the stage in London in 1955. In 1957 there was a production – in French – of *Fin de partie* at the Royal Court, London, and with it appeared *Acte sans paroles.* Novels such as *Molloy, Malone Meurt,* and *L'Innommable* were available, though not yet in English translations; and *Watt* (written in English) had been published in Paris in 1953. Pinter had in fact read a slightly abridged version of Chapter III of *Watt,*[5] presumably in 1951, and seems to have been influenced by it in the novel he was writing at the time, if one can work back from the evidence of his play *The Dwarfs,* based on this unpublished novel.[6] Pinter has in fact consistently and generously expressed his admiration for Beckett. In other words, in 1957, when Harold Pinter wrote his first three plays, Beckett was in the air, the Absurd was in the air, and waiting to be absorbed by a dramatist who was at once inexperienced, eager to experiment, and at the same time open to influence – though this last he is not normally anxious to concede.

Fundamentally, Pinter and Beckett are as dramatists quite unlike, Beckett the philosopher-playwright whose plays have been called "running commentaries on his novels"[7] and whose characters are Mankind, Pinter only occasionally and not very successfully essaying the philosopher, his plays rooted in an interest in how individuals will behave in given circumstances.

---

5. Published in *Irish Writing*, No. 17 (1951), under the title of "Extract from *Watt*".

6. See later, pp. 55 ff.

7. Richard N. Coe, *Beckett* (Edinburgh: Oliver and Boyd, 1964), p. 89.

I start writing a play from an image of a situation and a couple of characters involved, and these people remain for me quite real; if they were not, the play could not be written.[8]

It is not hard to see however why Beckett and the Absurd should fascinate the young playwright, particularly in those early days when insecurity dominated his plays to the exclusion of all other themes. Uncertainty is a very familiar landmark in the Beckett world. In Beckett's first and best-known play, *Waiting for Godot,* there is the basic uncertainty of whether or no Godot will turn up; Estragon does not know who beats him; neither Vladimir nor the boy is sure whether he is happy or sad; night comes not in the usual predictable earth-fashion but "pop! like that. . . just when we least expect it", and the tree bursts into leaf with comparable abruptness. Time is uncertain; none of the characters is ever certain what day it is, or even what part of the day, and Pozzo cries out:

Have you not done tormenting me with your accursed time?

Identity is uncertain. Names are called into question. Vladimir and Estragon are strangers in this part of the world; they have few identifying possessions, and their memories are partially, though not completely, defective. Towards the end of Act I, the Boy, messenger of Godot, asks what he is to say to Godot, and Vladimir replies:

Tell him. . . (*he hesitates.*) tell him you saw us. (*Pause.*) You did see us, didn't you?

But if the affinities between the uncertain worlds of Beckett and Pinter are obvious, so too are the disparities. The uncertainties of the Pinter world seem to be less deep-rooted, less extreme, than those of Beckett. Leaves in Pinter's world would certainly appear according to normal season and schedule; the characters in the early plays do not seriously question their own identity and existence (however confused their past history), though this does become one of the themes of the later and more difficult radio plays, *A Slight Ache* and *The Dwarfs.* There is also a difference in the area of uncertainty. The Beckett world is uncertain for the audience because it is uncertain for the characters; the Pinter

---

8. Harold Pinter, interview with Kenneth Tynan, B.B.C. Home Service, 28 October 1960. Quoted by Martin Esslin, *The Theatre of the Absurd.*

world is more uncertain for the audience than for the characters, because frequently the characters seem to be far more in the know about what is happening than we are. This suggests that Pinter's technique includes a certain amount of deliberate mystification, which is of course legitimate dramatic technique for heightening the audience's sense of fear and insecurity.

Uncertainty, whatever its nature, is a link between Pinter and not only Beckett but the drama of the Absurd in general; but is Pinter truly one of the Absurd? He has himself used the word "Absurd" in connection with his plays, Martin Esslin quotes him as saying:

> Everything is funny; the greatest earnestness is funny; even tragedy is funny. And I think what I try to do in my plays is to get this recognizable reality of the absurdity of what we do and how we behave and how we speak.9

Even now, when the wave of the Absurd seems in most places to be largely spent, "Absurd" is one of the more elastic words in the critical vocabulary, and it is not quite clear what Pinter himself means by it. He could be referring to the tragic-comic mood so wide-spread in contemporary literature, within the Absurd but also beyond it. Pinter is certainly conscious of the proximity of comedy and tragedy.

> The point about tragedy is that it is *no longer funny*. It is funny, and then it becomes no longer funny.10

His own plays are Absurd in this particular sense, in the juxtaposition of pathos and comedy. Pinter might also be referring to the "metaphysical anguish at the absurdity of the human condition", which Esslin suggests is the basic theme of major dramatists of the Absurd, such as Beckett, Adamov, Ionesco, and Genet;11 here Absurd is used in Ionesco's sense of "that which is devoid of purpose", pointless, senseless. Pinter's plays do not seem to be Absurd in this sense. They certainly suggest that life is uncertain, but not necessarily that it is also inevitably devoid of purpose, senseless, in the way that Beckett, Ionesco, Arrabal, Vian, Adamov, and Pinget, to name just a few, have implied. Perhaps the real

9. *The Theatre of the Absurd*, p. 211.

10. *Ibid.*, p. 212.

11. *Ibid.*, p. 17.

nigger in Pinter's woodpile, so far as being regarded as strictly a writer of the Absurd is concerned, is his basic allegiance to cause and effect, one's constant feeling even in the early plays that however bewildering and unexplained events may be they are by no means irrational. Ultimately, Pinter's plays are shaped by logic. To apply the description "Absurd" to them is surely to extend the usage of the word too loosely and imprecisely. In the long run, it probably does not matter very much whether we attach the label "Absurd" to Pinter's plays or not, except that thinking around the question may discourage us from blaming Pinter for failing to do what he has not been attempting, for failing in effect to be Beckett or Ionesco; Pinter has suffered from criticism of this kind, particularly as he moved away from writing plays which had at least some visible common bonds with the Absurd.

Though Pinter's Absurdity in these early plays may be questionable, his strength in the conventional skills of "good theatre," character presentation, and construction, is on much firmer ground. These conventional skills go a long way towards explaining why Pinter, though mildly avant-garde, has also achieved popular success – even the television hero Charlie Drake watched a Pinter play! Harold Pinter's skill in manipulating an audience may well be in part the result of his nine years as a repertory actor. He himself says:

> I had a pretty good notion in my earlier plays of what would shut an audience up; not so much what would make them laugh; that I had no ideas about.[12]

He quickly learned to shut the audience up with strong curtains, strong situations; the opposition of the victim against the terrifyingly unequal odds of the menace-figure is not, for instance, so very far removed from the similarly unbalanced contest between good and evil in melodrama, though the ending is different. Pinter denies us the emotional satisfaction of seeing those with whom we identify restored to health and prosperity, while evil is hissed off the stage or repentant. He also avoids the sentimentality of melodrama, coming closest to it, and quite suitably so, on occasions like Meg's tearful speech at Stanley's birthday party:

12. "Writing for Myself", *Twentieth Century*, CLXIX (February 1961), 172.

Well, I could cry because I'm so happy, having him here and not gone away, on his birthday, and there isn't anything I wouldn't do for him, and all you good people here tonight... (*She sobs.*)

Perhaps Aston's account of his experiences in the asylum in *The Caretaker* comes into this category of deliberate attack on the softer sentiments of the audience. From the beginning, Pinter punctuated his plays with moments of shock, moments where the unexpected may take one's breath away, simply because it is unexpected and, however harmless, for the time at least unknown. Rose, pottering around her room, opens the door to find Mr. and Mrs. Sands unexpectedly standing outside, and presumably the audience shares her fright until Mrs. Sands explains:

So sorry. We didn't mean to be standing here, like. Didn't mean to give you a fright. We've just come up the stairs.

There is a similar situation in *The Lover,* where Sarah opens the door to reveal not her lover as we had expected but John the milkman; for the audience there is a touch of fear in the brief confusion of the moment – unless of course they spring to the conclusion that John is the lover, in the tradition of the American iceman that cometh. Pinter is inclined to repeat anything that works, shock devices among them: the trick of plunging the stage into darkness, while the audience wonders what grim events are being enacted on it (*The Birthday Party* and *The Caretaker*), modified to blackouts of the television screen in *Tea Party*; the drum beat, pounding out Stanley's despair in *The Birthday Party,* suggesting mounting sexual passion in *The Lover*. The theatricality no doubt keeps audiences quiet; but in spite of his denials, Pinter also knew very well in those early plays how to make an audience laugh, for instance in the quietly irresistible opening scene of *The Birthday Party,* as Meg serves Petey his cornflakes and fried bread, and they discuss such items of interest as Lady Mary Splatt's new baby. There are moments of high comedy which are also sudden insights into terror or pathos ahead, such as the violent quarrel between Ben and Gus in *The Dumb Waiter* over the relative correctness of "light the kettle" and "light the gas". Comedy in Pinter frequently builds on the quicksands of fear; in seconds the hilarity of a birthday party (in which the audience joins) can slither into terrorization and madness. An interviewer once suggested to Pinter that

often an audience at your plays finds its laughter turning against
itself as it realizes what the situation in the play actually is.

Pinter agreed.

> I'm rarely consciously writing humour, but sometimes I find myself
> laughing at some particular point which has suddenly struck me as
> being funny. I agree that more often than not the speech only *seems*
> funny – the man in question is actually fighting a battle for his
> life.[13]

Pinter's early plays were not often discussed in terms of their
characterization, but his ability to suggest a personality, swiftly,
surely, often slightly caricatured, grotesque, is one of his most
formidable weapons in the theatre. He is interested in individuals
and their motives, as distinct from Mankind. John Russell Taylor
quotes him as saying specifically:

> ... I am interested primarily in people; I want to present living
> people to the audience, worthy of their interest primarily because
> they *are*, they exist, not because of any moral the author may draw
> from them.[14]

Of *The Caretaker,* Pinter says:

> At the end of *The Caretaker,* there are two people alone in a
> room, and one of them must go in such a way as to produce a sense
> of complete separation and finality. I thought originally that the
> play must end with the violent death of one at the hands of the
> other. But then I realised, when I got to the point, that the charac-
> ters as they had grown could never act this way. Characters always
> grow out of all proportion to your original conception of them,
> and if they don't the play is a bad one.[15]

One anecdote, related by Pinter in dialogue that could have come
from one of his plays, shows just how real the characters do
become to him:

> I had a terrible dream, after I'd written *The Caretaker,* about the
> two brothers. My house burned down in the dream, and I tried to
> find out who was responsible. I was led through all sorts of alleys
> and cafés and eventually I arrived at an inner room somewhere

13. "Harold Pinter", *Theatre at Work,* ed. Charles Marowitz and Simon
    Trussler (London: Methuen, 1967), pp. 107–8.

14. *Anger and After,* p. 244.

15. "Harold Pinter Replies", *New Theatre Magazine,* II (1961), 10.

and there were the two brothers from the play. And I said, so you burned down my house. They said don't be too worried about it, and I said I've got everything in there, everything, you don't realize what you've done, and they said it's all right, we'll compensate you for it, we'll look after you all right – the younger brother was talking – and thereupon I wrote them out a cheque for fifty quid – *I* gave *them* a cheque for fifty quid![16]

One the other hand, Pinter has never pretended omniscience where his characters are concerned, even in his final conception of them; he insisted early that the characters in a play need not be fully known to an audience, or indeed know themselves, which he saw as part of the more general problem of verification of reality. In a programme note for a performance of *The Room* and *The Dumb Waiter* at the Royal Court Theatre, London, in 1960, Pinter wrote:

The desire for verification is understandable but cannot always be satisfied. There are no hard distinctions between what is real and what is unreal, nor between what is true and what is false. The thing is not necessarily either true or false; it can be both true and false. The assumption that to verify what has happened and what is happening presents few problems I take to be inaccurate. A character on the stage who can present no convincing argument or information as to his past experience, his present behaviour or his aspirations, nor give a comprehensive analysis of his motives, is as legitimate and as worthy of attention as one who, alarmingly, can do all these things. The more acute the experience the less articulate its expression.

Harold Pinter sees his characters:

I write quite visually – I can say that. I watch the invisible faces quite closely. The characters take on a physical shape. I watch the faces as closely as I can. And the bodies.[17]

But even he does not know everything about them. Asked what Mick did for a living (in *The Caretaker*) he replied:

All I know is that whatever he did, he had his own van.[18]

– and one must admit that the fact that Mick owns his own van is a more important piece of information, in this play about struggles

---

16. *Theatre at Work*, p. 105.

17. "Two People in a Room", *New Yorker*, XLIII, No. 1 (25 February 1967), 36.

18. "Probing Pinter's Play", *Saturday Review*, L (8 April 1967), 97.

to possess, than details about what he did with it. In the early
plays, audiences are continually reminded that they do not know
everything about the characters. In later plays, such as *The Homecoming*, Pinter has modified his habit of mystery and presented a
few more facts about his characters; but not all. A great many
unanswered questions remain, nagging the imagination.

However, as we have now come to accept, fully documented
information about each character has very little to do with the
success or failure of characterization in a play, and quite often
lack of detailed information can actually be an asset. A character
in a play comes mysteriously alive when he says, or does, something which stirs the intellect, the imagination, or the emotions
of the audience, and there are a thousand and one different ways
of achieving this. A touch of enigma can be one of the most
useful methods of stirring audience imagination, as the popularity
of Hamlet testifies. What is important is not to tell all, but to
suggest that there is a great deal more that might be known.
Pinter's most memorable characters are those which come close
to caricature, vivid and grotesque, often almost Dickensian. The
best of them in these early plays are Goldberg, McCann, and Meg
of *The Birthday Party*. Pinter's method of suggesting such
characters is something like that of Dickens, though he cannot, as
Dickens so often does, crystallize character in a single, pithy
descriptive phrase. Like Dickens, Pinter seizes on a few outstanding characteristics, enlarges on them, repeats them over
and over. Uriah Heep constantly rubs hard, bony, clammy hands,
sees without appearing to look, smiles his hard, slit smile, and is
humble. In the same way, Goldberg's singular characteristics
are established and repeated. He makes his first appearance
carrying only a briefcase, followed by McCann with two suitcases
(immediately their relationship, in essence, is established), and
the first two lines of dialogue confirm Goldberg's dominance and
seemingly armour-plated self-confidence:

MCCANN Is this it?
GOLDBERG. This is it.
MCCANN. Are you sure?
GOLDBERG. Sure I'm sure... Sit back, McCann. Relax. What's
    the matter with you? I bring you down for a few days to the
    seaside. Take a holiday. Do yourself a favour. Learn to relax,
    McCann, or you'll never get anywhere.

Confident, often ridiculous, advice:

> The secret is breathing

– the habit of reminiscence that confuses rather than reveals, in Goldberg's stories of Uncle Barney, and of his three sons – the lightly sinister touch of the revelation about his sons:

> I lost my last two – in an accident

– the deliberate mystification of whether the surviving son is called Timmy or Manny – over all the unmistakable suggestion in Goldberg of the stage Jew – by the end of this first scene we have the outlines of a vivid, larger-than-life personality, seizing audience attention in every subsequent appearance on stage. Meg, though a simple person, is perhaps a more complex character study than Goldberg in the sense that we learn more about her, but even so her outstanding characteristics (motherly fussiness, slow mental processes, social standing) emerge in less than two pages, establishing Meg so surely that any actress would have within minutes at least a rough idea how she should be played. Pinter has described the real-life inspiration for Meg, and the situation of *The Birthday Party*:

> ... the other day a friend of mine gave me a letter I wrote to him in nineteen-fifty something, Christ knows when it was. This is what it says, "I have filthy insane digs, a great bulging scrag of a woman with breasts rolling at her belly, an obscene household, cats, dogs, filth, tea-strainers, mess, oh bullocks, talk, chat rubbish shit scratch dung poison, infantility, deficient order in the upper fretwork, fucking roll on..." Now the thing about this is *that* was *The Birthday Party* – I was in those digs, and this woman was Meg in the play, and there was a fellow staying there in East-bourne, on the coast. The whole thing remained with me, and three years later I wrote the play.[19]

Pinter's grotesques, like many of Dickens', are often powerfully single-minded (the mother in *A Night Out,* Davies in *The Caretaker,* and Max in *The Homecoming*) and, again like Dickens', both comic and terrifying for the same reasons, their gargoyle grotesqueness. Not all, of course; one would no more find Meg frightening than, for instance, Mrs. Micawber.

---

19. *Theatre at Work,* p. 98.

In these early plays Pinter had already lighted upon a particular technique of suggesting character that he was to rely on increasingly in the later plays: the revealing gesture, betraying motive or hidden tensions. In *The Birthday Party* it is used particularly with McCann, the stage Irishman to Goldberg's stage Jew. McCann says little, but there is a sense of repressed inner fires, hinted at in his terrifying concentration as he carefully tears newspapers into strips, not to be touched by Stanley, and with lengthy, terrible precision brushes his shoes. This suggestion of inner tension is verified not only in the interrogation scene but in his violent, if brief, attempt to confess Lulu:

> Kneel down woman and tell me the latest!

Stanley discloses the terrors he will not speak in his frantic beating of the birthday drum. In the latest three-act play, *The Homecoming,* Teddy and Lenny, locked in silent battle for Teddy's wife Ruth beneath a studiedly casual conversation, betray strain only in that the cigars of both men go out, unnoticed. Like the deliberate mystification and withholding of information, these revealing gestures set the audience imagination to work, insinuating that more is hidden, out of sight. On the other hand, the way characters speak, as well as the information they convey or fail to convey, is an important part of character-technique, and Pinter has been often and justly praised for his accurate ear for the way people talk, the repetitions, the non sequiturs of daily speech;[20] even here, even in its truth-to-life, Pinter dialogue, like Pinter characters, tends to be just a little larger than life, its repetitions and illogicalities and non sequiturs true – but faintly caricatured. How vital a role the Pinter grotesque character plays in the total effect of the play might be suggested by a comparison between *The Room* and *The Birthday Party*. *The Room* is a rather dull play, and one reason for its comparative lack of life is that the bulk of the dialogue is spoken by Rose, a dreary conversationalist. In many ways Meg of *The Birthday Party* is quite like Rose, with her insecurity, motherliness, and ambiguity of background. But Meg is heightened; she is at once funnier and more pathetic than Rose, and she is an important reason why *The Birthday Party* is a more lively play than *The Room,* though not of course the only

---

20. For discussion of Pinter's dialogue, see later, pp. 90 ff.

one. One could not pretend that the successful Pinter play owes its life entirely to its grotesque characters – Gus and Ben of *The Dumb Waiter* remain relatively vague, so that it is even difficult to guess how old they are, and *The Dumb Waiter* is a very successful farce, Ionesco style – but character, vivid and grotesque, has contributed a great deal to the richness and vitality of Pinter's major stage plays, *The Birthday Party, The Caretaker,* and *The Homecoming.*

From the beginning, Pinter has been praised for his skill in construction. He does not follow a set formula but prefers to experiment, with an increasing sureness of control. Pinter's first play, the one-act *The Room,* was rather crudely constructed on the principle of a many-layered sandwich. Rose remains stationary in the room, while other characters, Mr. and Mrs. Sands, Mrs. Kidd, and finally Riley, come and go, three times leaving her awkwardly on stage, filling in time with trivial stage business between visitors. The isolation of a character on stage can be used to considerable dramatic effect. If it is not too bizarre to set the medieval morality play *Everyman* beside *The Room,* one might remember how *Everyman* uses the isolation of the central character between "episodes" to considerable dramatic effect. In the morality play, Everyman stands alone on stage and speaks a soliloquy after each of his false friends, in the first half of the play, has failed him. Nothing could better suggest his isolation, the loneliness he dreads; by contrast, in the second half of the play, after Good Deeds has led him to Knowledge, he is not alone on stage again till he sinks into his grave. Something of this effect is perhaps achieved in *The Room,* a sense of Rose's vulnerability as she sits alone; but one tends to be rather more aware of the mechanical awkwardness of what is happening, the author's difficulty in getting his characters on and off the stage without their meeting in the doorway. Further, *The Room* does not always apportion its emphasis in a satisfying way. One of the funnier episodes is the one where Mr. and Mrs. Sands squabble over whether he will or will not sit down, his insistence to her that "you did not see me sit down because I did not sit bloody well down. I perched!" – leading to her firm statement "I didn't bring you into the world", and his brooding query, "well, who did then? That's what I want to know. Who did? Who did bring me into the world?" Though the scene is a foreshadowing of many

Pinter quarrels over the meaning of words, quarrels that are
actually about something quite different, it is an isolated comedy
sketch, not really integrated into the play. Another characteristic
Pinter touch is the monologue, found in most of the plays,
sometimes telling a story, sometimes springing unmistakably
from the old music hall monologue, as Peter Davison has suggested.[21] Pinter's powers of holding an audience through a long
speech are admirable. The long speech of *The Room* is Mrs.
Sands's description of how she and her husband came to look
for a place to live and found themselves in Rose's room. Its
length gives this speech an air of being crucial to the play, an
air of great weight and importance – not in fact justified by the
consequence of what is said. The author's rhetoric keeps one
listening, but in the end one is left with a feeling that stress has
been misplaced, almost incongruously. By contrast, Aston's long
speech in *The Caretaker* about his experiences in the asylum
shows how far Pinter's control has advanced. In *The Caretaker*
the weight of the unusually long speech is balanced by the importance of what is said: that is, the revelation of Aston, to some
extent "explaining" him (and all the more important because
of his previous reticence), and the turning point in his relationship
with the tramp Davies, his uncomprehending listener.

The structure of the one-act play, *The Dumb Waiter*, has no
such awkwardness. There is hardly an irrelevant line; comedy
and terror arise from the same situations, and mingle easily with
the familiar and the bizarre. The opening moments of the play
set the tone for what is to follow, the incongruous humour, the
suggestion of violence, as Ben and Gus react with horror and
distaste – "It's enough to make you want to puke, isn't it?"– to
the news items about the man of eighty-seven run over by a
lorry and the child of eight who killed a cat. The humour of
their reaction becomes in retrospect even funnier when we learn
the nature of Ben's and Gus's profession, and hear them calmly
discuss the technical details of it such as the looser texture of
women – "they don't seem to hold together like men." Information is unobtrusively conveyed, tension mounts; the bizarre
element becomes more and more fantastic. Comic touches (the

21. "Contemporary Drama and Popular Dramatic Forms", *Aspects of Drama
and the Theatre* (Sydney: Sydney University Press, 1965), pp. 145–97.

lavatory with the delayed action flush, the sheets that pong, the gas-kettle battle, and the earlier intrusions of the dumb waiter) recur at carefully spaced intervals, until Gus discovers that he has a headache. From this point, the first hint of Gus's physical disintegration, the comedy begins to fall away. Towards the end of the play comes an echo of the opening, significantly changed. Ben looks at the paper he is holding and exclaims over it very much as he did in the opening scene when he was reading the sensational items to Gus, but this time does not actually read aloud. Gus, subdued, replies as if Ben were speaking the words, and ends, as he did in the first exchange, with:

Incredible.

This time, however, the stage directions tell us he is "almost inaudible".

The Birthday Party, a three-act play with a larger cast than *The Dumb Waiter,* is more complex in structure. It follows a conventional three-act pattern, with markedly strong curtains for Act I and Act II. The end of Act I, the drum-beating scene, makes clear Stanley's recognition of the fate that awaits him; the end of Act II is the horrifying culmination of the birthday party, with Stanley backed up against the wall, giggling, the light from the torch held by McCann lighting up his face in the darkness, while Goldberg and McCann converge upon him. Act III begins with an echo of the opening scene of the play; like the echo of *The Dumb Waiter,* it is a repetition with marked, and sobering, differences. It is breakfast time once again, and Petey is reading his newspaper; but Meg has run out of cornflakes and the two gentlemen "had the last of the fry this morning". Meg and Petey both sound flat and subdued, and Meg has a splitting headache. If there is a weakness in the structure of *The Birthday Party,* it is in the third act. Every episode in it could be justified: the suggestion of life going on as usual in the repeated breakfast scene – the revelation that Goldberg is not invulnerable and infallible, in the scene where he tells McCann the secret of his success – Lulu's admission that she knows something is wrong:

An old woman nearly killed and a man gone mad – How can I go back behind that counter now? Oh Nat, why did you do it?

– the visible proof of Stanley's collapse, when McCann brings him on stage in striped trousers, black jacket, white collar, and bowler hat, unable to speak, showing no reaction when they *"woo him, gently and with relish"* with promises of a glorious future – and, finally, the conversation between Meg and Petey at the end of the play, making plain that they intend to close their eyes to what has happened. Dramatically, however, this third act is a slow slide downhill, lacking the tension of the earlier scenes. The crisis is over, and what follows is almost an anticlimax. In his subsequent stage play, *The Caretaker,* for Pinter (as for many contemporary dramatists) the third act remained a problem, one he seems to have solved ingeniously and finally in *The Homecoming* – by simply omitting Act III altogether.

2 the radio plays: a slight ache, the dwarfs, a night out

Harold Pinter has to date written three radio plays: *A Slight Ache* (1959), *The Dwarfs* (1960), and *A Night Out* (1960). A television version of *A Night Out* followed two months after the original radio broadcast. A television play, *Night School,* was also broadcast in 1960, and for several years was not published. Pinter's reason for deciding at the time not to publish it was quite simple. *Night School,* according to Pinter, contains

> characteristics that implied I was slipping into a formula. It so happens that this was the worst thing I have written. The words and ideas have become automatic, redundant. That was the red light for me, and I don't feel that I shall fall into that pit again.[1]

Then, in 1966, a radio version of *Night School* was broadcast on the Third Programme (with two additional minor characters), and in 1967 this radio adaptation was published in the same volume as the television plays *Tea Party* and *The Basement.* It would perhaps be unduly harsh to suggest that Pinter's earlier decision not to publish *Night School* was the right one, but even in its revised

---

1. "Harold Pinter Replies", interview with Harry Thompson, *New Theatre Magazine,* II (1961), 9–10.

form the play does not come anywhere near his best. Walter, a young man just released from prison, is righteously indignant to find that the elderly aunts with whom he lives when he is not in prison (for Walter is a persistent though depressingly unsuccessful crook) have let his room. The new tenant is an attractive girl, a schoolteacher, who has made the room "really pretty", uses perfume, leaves the bath "good as new", and goes to night school three times a week. Walter sets out to dislodge the intruder. A photograph rouses his suspicions that the "night school" is in fact a nightclub where she is an entertainer. Walter deviously sets on her trail the elderly landlord Mr. Solto, who invites her to visit his beach house and watch the waves in the moonlight. As the play ends, the old ladies are surprised to find that their tenant has disappeared in the middle of the night, leaving a brief note of farewell. For once, the expulsion does not seem to matter much; Sally, the victim of the plot, is apparently well able to take care of herself – in which she is probably unique among the Pinter vanquished. It is not a very convincing play, and perhaps the best things in it are the two elderly aunts, Annie and Milly, like all Pinter's old women grotesquely alive; and the expansive Mr. Solto, blood brother to Goldberg of *The Birthday Party*.

The confrontation of Harold Pinter and the medium of radio was fraught with interesting possibilities. In his earlier plays, Pinter had already shown a dogged interest in experimenting, in spite of lack of understanding from many audiences and critics. The particular radio channel for which Pinter wrote *A Slight Ache, A Night Out,* and *The Dwarfs* was the B.B.C. Third Programme – the Third Programme which commissioned Samuel Beckett's *All That Fall* and which has surely an unequalled reputation for giving its writers freedom to explore, and freedom to ignore any demands of catering for wide popular taste. Pinter said later:

> When I wrote *The Dwarfs* a few months ago, I was able to experiment in form – a mobile, flexible structure, more flexible and mobile than in any other medium. And from the point of view of content, I was able to go the whole hog and enjoy myself exploring to a degree which wouldn't be acceptable in any other medium.[2]

---

2. *Twentieth Century,* CLXIX (February 1961), 172.

However, Pinter's first three plays would have suggested that he was instinctively a stage playwright, with a strong feeling for visual, theatrical effects, all of which were lost to him when he turned to radio. Instead, the playwright was left with a medium whose essential characteristics are intimacy, flexibility, and the enormous responsibility of the spoken word.

In his radio plays, Pinter abandoned the single room setting. One could well suspect that as a practical man of the theatre he has always recognized the economic usefulness of the single set, as well as its symbolic significance. Certainly he has returned to the room setting in all later stage plays to date, but invariably in his radio and television dramas, the characters have been allowed to wander. In radio particularly, there is not much point, either economic or symbolic, in confining one's characters to a single setting.[3] The setting of *A Slight Ache* is quite flexible, wandering through various rooms of a country house, from scullery to study; it is indicated that there is also a view of a "large well kept garden" with "flower beds, trimmed hedges, etc." *A Night Out* allows the characters complete freedom of movement, ranging from the kitchen of the house occupied by Albert Stokes and his mother to the home of Albert's employer, Mr. King, taking in a coffee stall and a prostitute's bedroom, and ending where it began, in the Stokes's kitchen – a very suitable pattern for a play which shows a young man's attempt to escape from his mother's clutches and ends, fruitlessly, in his being more hedged in than ever. The setting of *The Dwarfs* is simply not important, and it is not surprising that even the author is rather forgetful

---

3. *A Slight Ache, The Dwarfs,* and *A Night Out* are published in one volume, *A Slight Ache and Other Plays* (London: Methuen, 1961); as published, only *The Dwarfs* appears in its original radio form. *A Night Out* is printed in the television version that followed soon after the first radio broadcast, and *A Slight Ache* has been somewhat cursorily adapted for the stage. There are few vital changes; the additional "stage directions" in the printed versions of *A Slight Ache* and *A Night Out* are for the most part either descriptions of actions already implicit in the dialogue or else production suggestions, presumably added to help the reader imagine the scene. Only at one point does a stage direction make a significant difference. In the radio version of *A Night Out* we have to take Albert's word that he did not touch Eileen, as she thinks; in the published television version it is made quite clear that he is guiltless, and it was old Mr. Ryan's hand that strayed. *A Slight Ache* retains a few purely radio directions such as *"Fade out and silence"*, which give a rather hybrid and uneasy feeling to the script when it is read.

in describing it. The stage directions at the beginning tell us
that "the action of the play moves from Mark's house to Len's
house in a London suburb". This quite ignores the fact that the
ending of the play also moves into the street, with "steps on the
road", and then into a hospital.

On first impression, it might seem that though the single room
setting has disappeared. *A Slight Ache* is yet another drama of
the invasion of menace, menace this time in the person of the
Matchseller, an old man who for two months has been standing
constantly outside the back gate of Edward and Flora's country
house, without apparently making a single sale of his wares. His
presence may have a perfectly reasonable explanation, but at no
point in the play is it explained. Like the earlier Pinter agents of
menace he remains enigmatic, perhaps even more enigmatic than
they are, because during the play he speaks not a word, though
according to Edward he is not untouched by what is happening;
it is difficult to tell, however, whether he is weeping, or laughing,
or both, as Edward and Flora pour over him a steady stream of
words, voluble and revealing. Edward at first thinks the Matchseller has been laughing at him, then is moved to discover that he
has apparently been mistaken:

> You haven't been laughing. You're crying. (*Pause.*) You're weeping.
> You're shaking with grief. For me. I can't believe it. For my plight.
> I've been wrong.

Yet is he wrong? The play ends with the collapse of Edward into
a physical inertia very much like that of the earlier Pinter victims,
as he passively accepts the Matchseller's tray which Flora places
in his hands before she leads the Matchseller triumphantly into
the garden. If this is another comedy of menace, it is menace
with a difference. For the first time there is no suggestion of a
higher power looming behind the agent, no father, Monty, or
Wilson. In addition, for the first time the victims, Edward and
Flora, bring the menace into the house themselves, unlike the
victims of the earlier plays, particularly *The Room* and *The
Birthday Party,* where Riley, Goldberg, and McCann sought out
their unwilling prey; and when the menace is finally installed in
the house, he continues to play a completely passive role, all the
action being taken by the seeming victims, Edward who destroys
himself, Flora who finds new life.

The vision of man destroying himself in the presence of a threat that remains passive, inactive, is not new in modern literature; one thinks immediately, for instance, of Kafka's novels. Pinter's plays have frequently been related to the Kafka novels, particularly *The Birthday Party,* where Goldberg and McCann have been compared with the two men who come, in *The Trial,* to arrest Joseph K.:

> Someone must have been telling lies about Joseph K., for without having done anything wrong he was arrested one fine morning.

For the most part the relationship between the two writers is fairly general, though Pinter has acknowledged Kafka's influence; both show man crushed by unexplained, mysterious outside forces, both have an eye for the comic-terrifying, and for grotesque character. But in *A Slight Ache* there is a deeper affinity between Kafka and Pinter, in that Kafka too sees man destroying himself before a menace that is a menace only because he regards it as such. Even though the two warders in the beginning invade K.'s house in *The Trial,* it is K. who after this initial intrusion seeks his own trial. He says "it is only a trial if I recognize it as such", and he knows that "he had received the defeat only because he had insisted on giving battle". This would seem to be true also of Pinter's Edward in *A Slight Ache,* but not of his earlier victims of menace.

Affinities between *A Slight Ache* and Kafka's second celebrated novel *The Castle* are even closer. Kafka emphasizes that the Castle is not in appearance impressive or frightening. When K. first sees it he is

> ... disappointed in the castle; it was after all only a wretched-looking town, a huddle of village houses, whose sole merit, if any, lay in being built of stone, but the plaster had long since flaked off and the stone seemed to be crumbling away. K. had a fleeting recollection of his native town. It was hardly inferior to this so-called Castle, and if it were merely a question of enjoying the view it was a pity to have come so far. K. would have done better to visit his native town again, which he had not seen for such a long time.

In spite of its unimpressive appearance, the Castle exerts an enormous if passive destructive power. In its shadow the characters destroy themselves. The punishment of Amalia and her family,

after Amalia has rejected a Castle official, seems self-inflicted;
her sister Olga explains to K. that if the family had themselves
come out into the village, and shown by their attitudes that the
incident was closed, the whole business would have been over;
but this they do not seem able to do, and instead plunge deeper
and deeper into suffering and ostracism. The Castle itself
remains silent and passive:

> ... while we couldn't help noticing the ostracism of the village,
> the Castle gave us no sign. Of course we had no sign of favour
> from the Castle in the past, so how could we notice the reverse?
> This blankness was worst of all.

There seems to be no reason why K. should not simply leave the
village and the Castle and his former life (just as there seems to
be no tangible reason why Vladimir and Estragon should not give
up their long wait for Godot and go somewhere else), but instead
K. stays and slowly destroys himself before it.

Pinter establishes early that the Matchseller is old, weak, and
harmless-seeming; Flora says he is a "quiet, harmless old man,
going about his business. He's quite harmless", and "I'm not sure
if he can hear, or even see." His few actions in the play emphasize
the suggestion of weakness; he stumbles and sits, drops the tray
of matches. Flora even suggests that he is "weak in the head".
Yet his passive presence brings on Edward's self-destruction.

One might also be reminded of Ionesco's play *The Killer,* in
which the hero, Bérenger, similarly pursues his silent menace, the
Killer, and in effect destroys himself before this menace, even
though it is the Killer who finally draws the knife. Ionesco's
menace-figure is hardly physically impressive or frightening; he
is described as "very small and puny, with a torn hat on his head
and a shabby old gaberdine; he has only one eye, which shines
with a steely glitter, and a set expression on his still face; his toes
peeping out of the holes in his old shoes." So unimportant is his
physical appearance that there is a possibility that he may not
exist at all:

> ... or possibly there is no Killer at all. Bérenger could be talking
> to himself, alone in the half-light.

Bérenger, before he collapses into Pinter-like inertia, aims at the
Killer (if he exists) two loaded pistols, underlining his physical
advantage; but of course does not fire. In the final scene, the Killer

stands silent, with only an occasional sinister chuckle, while Bérenger pours forth floods of words, sometimes like Edward descending to crude abuse –

> You filthy dirty moronic imbecile! You're ugly as a monkey! Fierce as a tiger, stupid as a mule...

– but in effect dredging up his own inner weaknesses, discovering in his flow of words the shallowness of his own being and the triteness of his thought, exactly as Edward does. Bérenger constantly finds "reasons" to excuse the irrational brutality of the Killer, preferring to be victim rather than to take positive action to save himself. The process of Bérenger's disintegration is reminiscent of Edward's; an important difference, however, is that through Bérenger Ionesco is making a social and political comment of a kind foreign to Pinter.

Finally, one might think of a play which, though a long way from the Absurd, is shaped on a comparable pattern of man's self-destruction: Archibald MacLeish's *The Fall of the City,* which ends with a whole city prostrating itself before – a suit of empty armour.

Though the situation is at its most extreme in *A Slight Ache,* dominance in Pinter is frequently equated with silence, with passivity that is almost contempt. Stanley in *The Birthday Party* talks volubly and vainly at the monosyllabic McCann, trying to persuade him that he is someone else; Aston turns his back, in silence, when Davies at the end of *The Caretaker* pleads brokenly for another chance; Lenny in *The Homecoming* allows his aged father to rage impotently and lengthily, his own contemptuous self-assurance needing few words; in *The Basement,* Stott and Jane, in silence ignoring Law, retire to Law's bed to make love, and Law's futile attempts to keep the conversation going falter and die. In the Pinter world, it often happens that A may become dominant by remaining passive, while B, frantically active, gradually loses ascendancy. This pattern of reversal of dominance Pinter explores in *A Slight Ache* and in the short story whose movement is very similar – the story already mentioned, *The Examination.*

In both story and play, two men are brought together in a room, which in the beginning "belongs" to one of them, ownership which gives him initial superiority. The "I" narrator of *The Examination* tells us:

Yet I was naturally dominant, by virtue of my owning the room.

and Edward also believes that ownership of the room confers certain rights:

> God damn it, I'm entitled to know something about you! You're in my blasted house, on my territory, drinking my wine, eating my duck! Now you've had your fill you sit like a hump, a mouldering heap. In my room. My den.

Rose in *The Room* and all three characters of *The Caretaker* would understand precisely what the narrator and Edward were talking about.

Edward in *A Slight Ache* talks incessantly, sometimes questioning the Matchseller, sometimes simply revealing himself. The Matchseller is quite silent, but Edward does not regard his silence as non-communication, and insists to Flora after some little time that he has discovered certain facts about his guest, and hopes to learn more.

> He's had various trades, that's certain. His place of residence is unsure. He's. . .he's not a drinking man. As yet, I haven't discovered the reason for his arrival here. I shall in due course. . .by nightfall.

A similar situation exists apparently in *The Examination,* where the narrator tells us:

> When Kullus was disposed to silence I invariably acquiesced, and prided myself on those occasions with tactical acumen. But I did not regard these silences as intervals, for they were not, and neither, I think, did Kullus so regard them. For if Kullus fell silent, he did not cease to participate in our examination. Never, at any time, had I reason to doubt his active participation, through word and through silence, between interval and interval, and I recognized what I took to be his devotion as actual and unequivocal, besides, as it seemed to me, obligatory.

Both Kullus and the Matchseller remain inscrutable, and it is on this inscrutability that their interrogators founder. In *The Examination*:

> For he journeyed from silence to silence, and I had no course but to follow. Kullus's silence, where he was entitled to silence, was compounded of numerous characteristics, the which I duly noted. But I could not always follow his course, and where I could not follow, I was no longer his dominant.

Later, admits the narrator, "his inconsistencies began to cause me alarm, and his silence to confound me". Edward in *A Slight Ache* is also baffled by his listener's seeming inconsistency; he cannot tell if he is weeping or laughing. His confusion is actually greater than that of the narrator in *The Examination* – there seems little doubt that at least the narrator knows who Kullus is, but this simple knowledge of the identity of his partner is denied to Edward. For the narrator and Edward both, the situation ends in total defeat at the hands of their passive partners, and a complete reversal of their positions.

> And so the time came when Kullus initiated the intervals at his own inclination, and pursued his courses at will, and I was able to remark some consistency in his behaviour. For now I followed him in his courses without difficulty, and there was no special duration for interval or examination, but one duration, in which I participated. My devotion was actual and unequivocal. I extended my voluntary co-operation, and made no objection to procedure. For I desired a summation of our efforts. And when Kullus remarked the absence of a flame in the grate, I was bound to acknowledge this. And when he remarked the presence of a stool, I was equally bound. And when he removed the blackboard, I offered no criticism. And when he closed the curtains, I did not object.
>
> For we were now in Kullus's room.

Edward, more simply, accepts silently the tray of matches which Flora hands to him.

One difference in the pattern, however, is that in *The Examination* it is hinted that it has all happened before: even when the narrator is in the dominant position he remembers the time when the room belonged to Kullus. Will it happen again, one asks, and again and yet again? No such suggestion is made in *A Slight Ache,* but it is to recur in *The Basement*.

It could be tempting to see this play solely in terms of the destruction of Edward, because he is the more dominant, complex, and interesting character, and he happens to be on stage for a greater length of time than his wife; such a view would bring the play more closely in line with the comedies of menace. But *A Slight Ache* does also contain Flora, who is not merely part of the background, as we might say of Meg in *The Birthday Party,* but an active participant. *A Slight Ache* is only in part about

Edward's self-destruction; the play as a whole shows how two people react in totally different ways to the same deliberately negative force or being (like Ionesco's Killer, possibly he does not exist at all?) and under pressure of his presence, reveal themselves, and the nature of their relationship.

We learn a little about Edward and Flora and their uneasy relationship before the Matchseller enters their lives, in a deftly informative opening scene. We find that they live so quietly that the killing of a wasp, trapped in the marmalade jar, is an adventure; that Edward is the kind of man who needs a canopy to shelter him from the sun, in the garden; that he will argue bitterly with his wife over trivial terminology, whether wasps bite or sting –

If you don't stop saying that word I shall leave this table

– but is not able to attach the right names to the right plants in his garden, unlike the more practical Flora (he thinks that the honeysuckle is "convolvulus, or something", and that the convolvulus is japonica). It is symptomatic of the chasm between them that they have not in two months mentioned the mysterious Matchseller standing outside their gate, in sun and storm – "A summer storm. He stood without moving, while it raged about him" – although Edward is intensely afraid of him, so much so that in the two months of the Matchseller's presence "I haven't been able to step outside the back gate". Flora on the other hand has decided that he is "a very nice old man, really". In their reactions to the Matchseller they reveal themselves more deeply. Flora remains simple, uncomplicated, to the end, though the inner woman proves to be rather different from our initial impression. With Edward, a more complex character, we strike a problem of language that is to be even more marked in *The Dwarfs*. In these two plays, written without the pressure of catering for popular taste, Pinter's leading characters become obscure in expression; the more deeply they reveal themselves, the more they attempt to speak out their inmost concerns, the more private the symbolism and language they use. Edward's dialogue in *A Slight Ache* begins simply enough, but as the pressure on him intensifies he seems increasingly to be speaking of a private vision not clearly communicated to us.

Edward's first diagnosis of the Matchseller tells us little about the Matchseller, but gives a hint of the problem that is destroying

Edward's own peace of mind, and which shapes his reaction to the Matchseller's presence. He tells Flora:

> The bastard isn't a matchseller at all. Curious I never realized that before. He's an impostor.

Edward might well suspect that he himself is in a sense an impostor, in that he is living a second-hand life, as a man who writes about the tropical phenomena of Africa but has never been there –

> I understand in the Gobi Desert you can come across some very strange sights. Never been there myself. Studied the maps though. Fascinating things, maps.

– and who, though he annually entertains the villagers and believes he has their regard, is not actually the squire. More broadly, Edward, like Len in *The Dwarfs,* seems to be preoccupied with the problem of identity, superficially with the identity of the Matchseller only, but more deeply with his own identity, his own existence, perhaps the very existence of a universe beyond himself, and the difficulties of perceiving it accurately. His preoccupation with this problem comes through in his two separate interviews with the Matchseller, interviews which differ in tone, but follow a similar pattern of development.

These interviews take place in Edward's study after Flora, on Edward's insistence, has reluctantly brought the Matchseller into the house. The first begins with Edward's conventional attempt to make the guest feel at home, the offer of a chair and a drink – "Sit down, old man. What will you have? Sherry? Or what about a double scotch?" The dialogue that follows is partly trivial social chatter, on such absorbing topics as the late squire and his family – "Nice old man he was. Great chess-player, as I remember. Three daughters. The pride of the county" – and partly quite superficial questions such as "Do you live in the village?" and "Do you find it chilly in here?" The Matchseller remains silent and inscrutable; Edward at first shows signs of irritation, then becomes brutally insolent, telling the Matchseller:

> You disgust me, quite forcibly, if you want to know the truth.

Suddenly his irritation collapses and he asks (the stage directions say "in a low voice"):

> I want to ask you a question. Why do you stand outside my back

gate, from dawn to dusk, why do you pretend to sell matches, why. . .?

To emphasize the importance of the question, not of course answered, the Matchseller begins to shiver and sag, and stumbles into a chair, while Edward himself, "with great weariness", goes into the garden for some fresh air. In his absence, Flora talks to the Matchseller, tells him about the poacher who raped her when she was a girl, asks him "Do you ever. . . think about women?" and says seductively "Tell me about love. Speak to me of love." Like Edward, she can be insulting – "I'm sure you must have been quite attractive once. . . Not any more, of course. You've got a vile smell" – but she has decided to keep the Matchseller, and buy him "little toys to play with. On your deathbed." – after of course he has been given "a lovely lathery bath. And a good scrub."

Edward's subsequent, second interview with the Matchseller begins, like the first, with a social attempt to make him feel at home; but the play is moving further and further away from naturalism, and the familiar invitation to have a drink now becomes:

> Take off all your togs, if you like. Make yourself at home. Strip to the buff. Do as you would in your own house.

The tone is different; at the beginning of the first interview, Edward speaks "cheerfully", according to stage directions; in the second, he speaks "coolly". The moment he finally loses his ascendancy over the Matchseller is the moment he admits the ridiculousness of his fussily ordered life with its illusion of stability, nostalgically remembered in "I could pour hot water down the spout hole,[4] yes, easily, no difficulty, my grasp firm, my command established, my life accounted for. . ." In defeat, sensing or imagining that the Matchseller is laughing at him, Edward admits:

> Yes, yes, you're quite right, it is funny.
> (*Pause. He drops his arms.*)
> Laugh your bloody head off! Go on. Don't mind me. No need to be polite.

---

4. Referring to the epic battle with the wasp, which Edward finally subdued by pouring hot water down the hole of the marmalade jar in which it had become trapped.

Why did Edward invite the Matchseller into the room? Was it "in order to determine your resemblance to – some other person?" He suggests the difficulty of perceiving an external object accurately:

> ... In fact every time I have seen you you have looked quite different to the time before.
> (*Pause.*)
> Admitted that sometimes I viewed you through dark glasses, yes, and sometimes through light glasses, and on other occasions bare eyed, on other occasions through the bars of the scullery window, or from the roof, yes in driving snow, or from the bottom of the drive in thick fog, or from the roof again in blinding sun, so blinding, so hot, that I had to skip and jump and bounce in order to remain in one place.

And then:

> Not that I had any difficulty in seeing you, no, no, it was not so much my sight, my sight is excellent – in winter I run about with nothing on but a pair of polo shorts – no it was not so much deficiency in my sight as the airs between me and my object – don't weep – the change of air, the currents obtaining in the space between me and my object, the shades they make, the shapes they take, the quivering, the eternal quivering – please stop crying – nothing to do with the heat-haze.

Finally Edward speaks his last, crucial and unanswered question (the stage directions say "with great, final effort – a whisper"):

> Who are you?

He does not speak again. Throughout the play, Edward has flirted with the idea of identifying himself with the Matchseller; at the end of the play, it would seem they have changed identities. Which is Edward? Which is the Matchseller? It might also be relevant that Edward's most intense and vividly expressed memory is of a moment of complete passivity; and passivity is one of the characteristics of the Matchseller, a passivity so complete that in the storm he "remained quite still, while it thundered all about him". Edward remembers his experience when

> ... I lay on my side in my polo shorts, my fingers lightly in contact with the blades of grass, the earthflowers, the petals of the earth-flowers flaking, lying on my palm, the underside of all the great foliage dark, above me, but it is only afterwards I say the foliage was dark, the petals flaking, then I said nothing, things happened

upon me, then in my times of shelter, the shades, the petals,
carried themselves, carried their bodies upon me, and nothing
entered my nook, nothing left it.

Flora also reveals herself under the pressure of the Matchseller's
presence, a Flora rather different from the seemingly conventional
tea-pouring Englishwoman of the first scene. Pinter's portrait of
her is simpler than that of Edward; she emerges as the dissatisfied
wife, the woman who has longed apparently in vain for children.
(One notes Edward's ambiguous comment on the Matchseller:

You're no more disgusting than Fanny, the squire's daughter, after
all. In appearance you differ but not in essence. There's the same...

Flora's reaction to the Matchseller is the exact opposite to Edward's.
Edward breaks when the Matchseller's presence reveals to him
the inadequacies of his life; Flora, equally made conscious of
inadequacies by the Matchseller, simply takes over the strange
guest to compensate for these deficiencies, and proceeds to turn
him into the husband and child she has, apparently, been denied.
The opposition of their attitudes is sharply underlined in two
lines of dialogue near the end of the play. As Edward asks the
Matchseller:

Who are you?

Flora is heard calling, off stage:

Barnabas?

She neither knows nor cares who he is, but has simply given him
a name, as well as a role to fill; and it is a name which means,
with deliberate or accidental significance, "the son of consolation".[5]

If *A Slight Ache* suggested that Pinter was discarding the
pattern of invasion of menace from without, it also heralded the
beginning of a new pattern, one which was to dominate the 1959–
1960 plays: the expulsion of one member of a triangular relationship. This is not to say that every play from this period followed
the formula; *Night School* ends with the expulsion of Sally but
the play has a cast of six, while *A Night Out,* which has a larger

---

5. In "Pinter's *A Slight Ache* as Ritual", *Modern Drama,* XI (December 1968),
   334, Katherine H. Burkman points out that "the day of Saint Barnabas,
   June eleventh in the old-style calendar, was the day of the summer solstice,
   while Barnaby-bright is the name for the longest day and the shortest night
   of the year".

cast than any other Pinter play to date (fifteen characters), tells of Alfred's desperate attempts to break from a strangling bond with his mother, an attempt which ends with the bond winding tighter than ever. However, *A Slight Ache, The Dwarfs,* and the stage play of the period, *The Caretaker,* all have casts of three people; and at the end of each play a character who believed himself secure is excluded, on the outside.

The Dwarfs, Pinter's notoriously "difficult" play, was apparently dramatized from an early unpublished novel by Pinter, in which there was an extra character, a girl, excised from the radio play.[6] There is very little "plot" in *The Dwarfs.* The three characters are Len and his two friends, Pete and Mark; in the background are the dwarfs, seen apparently only by Len, unattractive beings who "scrub their veins at the running sink" and eat "in a chuckle of fingers. Backchat of bone, crosstalk of bristled skin." They appear in the play solely through Len's descriptions of them. Our first impression is that Len is the link between his friends Mark and Pete, that he knows both of them better than they know each other. This impression rises partly from the construction of the play; until near the end of it we hear Len talking with Pete, then Len with Mark (interspersed with monologues by Len) in rotation, but not Mark and Pete together. We see Pete and Mark largely through Len's eyes, vividly described in monologue, Pete the cruel, who tells Len that "you're a homicidal maniac", and is identified by Len with the gull tearing the rat to pieces:

> Pete walks by the river. . . .Slicing gull. Gull. Down. He stops. Stone. Watches. Rat corpse in the yellow grass. Gull pads. Gull probes. Gull stamps his feet. Gull whinnies up. Gull screams, tears, Pete tears, digs, Pete cuts, breaks, Pete stretches the corpse, flaps his wings, Pete's beak grows, probes, digs, pulls, the river jolts, no moon. . .

Mark the sensual:

> Mark sits by the fireside. Crosses his legs. His fingers wear a ring. The finger poised. Mark regards his finger. He regards his legs. He regards the fireplace. Outside the door is the black blossom. He combs his hair with an ebony comb.

There is a hint of interest between Mark and Pete, however, Mark

---

6. J.R. Taylor, *Anger and After* (London: Methuen, 1962), p. 255.

tells Len that he spends too much time with Pete, Pete tells Len that he spends too much time with Mark; each implies that the other will do Len no good, but that "I can handle him". Halfway through the play, the balance of friendship changes, and Len is excluded from the new intimacy of Mark and Pete. The crucial scene of the change occurs off-stage, as it were, and is described by Len with vivid economy, in a kind of free verse speech; as Pete and Mark talk, Len tries to join in the conversation and is ignored:

> I speak, from a squatting position. No one replies.
> I stand on my hands. They glance. They talk.

As the reversal of loyalties proceeds on its inevitable way, Len comments:

> Both of you bastards, you've made a hole in my side, I can't plug it! (*Pause.*) I've lost a kingdom.

A reference to the Knight, the only chess man to move always over another, might remind one of Beckett's chess devices in *Endgame*, as Len says:

> He may be your black Knight, you may be his Black Knight, that's friendship, that's this that I know.

The conclusion is briefly recorded. Pete and Mark are now heard exchanging dialogue; they visit together Len who is in hospital, and Len is the outsider in not knowing that Mark now smokes a pipe. Mark tells him that "we've been walking up the street back to back" and in a sudden flash of jealousy Len orders them not to sit on his bed:

> You're supposed to sit on the chairs.

The dwarfs also leave Len:

> It's insupportable. I'm left in the lurch. Not even a stale frank-furter, a slice of bacon rind, a leaf of cabbage, not even a mouldy piece of salami, like they used to sling me in the days when we told old tales by suntime.

An obviously important, and difficult, question in under-standing the play is: who or what are the dwarfs? Pervasive beings, we are never allowed to forget them for long, as they watch Len and his friends, or go on picnics, leaving Len "to sweep the yard, pacify the rats". When they return from these excursions,

I tell them I've slaved like a martyr, I've skivvied till I was black in the face, what about a tip, what about the promise of a bonus, what about a little something? They yawn, they show the blood stuck between their teeth, they play their scratching game, they tongue their chops, they bring in their nets, their webs, their traps, they make monsters of their innocent catch, they gorge. Countless diversions.

Suggested interpretations of the "meaning" of the dwarfs have included the possibility that they are financial barons; the added dimension of the poetic imagination (which Len loses at the end of the play, as Aston of *The Caretaker* loses his in the asylum); the unseen masters of the world; and "some dwarfs which one of the characters imagines in the yard", as an early reviewer put it.

It is important to mark the circumstances in which the dwarfs first appear in the play, and when they leave. Each appearance of these hideous beings seems to be linked with the disintegration of the relationship between Len and his two friends. They first appear after Pete has warned Len against seeing too much of Mark, and related his dream of corrupt and peeling flesh, the panic in the tube station when the skin of everyone in the crowd begins "dropping off like lumps of cats' meat". The dwarfs come for a special reason, for a special job:

They clock in very early, scenting the event. They are like kites in a city disguise. . . They're on the spot with no time wasted and circle the danger area.

Len will watch with the dwarfs; and so, with due warning from them, "I shall be able to clear my stocks, should there be a landslide". Apart from such diversions as holding picnics and playing with beetles and twigs, the dwarfs keep a careful eye on Len's friends, and the long descriptions of Pete, the gull, and Mark by the fireside are each accompanied by a reference to the watching, capable, industrious dwarfs. The moment the dwarfs choose to leave Len is the moment when the relationship between him, Pete, and Mark is finally severed, leaving Len alone, on the outside. Gone with them is the litter of the yard, "scraps of cats' meat, pig bollocks, tin cans, bird brains, spare parts of all the little animals, a squelching squealing carpet . . ." Is it possible that these dwarfs represent, not the poetic imagination, and not the unseen rulers of the world, but simply the miseries, jealousies, and ignoblenesses of the dissolving relationship, ending when the relationship itself ends, leaving Len in the antiseptic state of dead emotions?

> Now all is bare. All is clean. All is scrubbed. There is a lawn. There is a shrub. There is a flower.

Such an interpretation would also explain why the dwarfs seem to Len to be "anticipating a rarer dish, a choicer spread". Immediately preceding Len's last left-in-the-lurch monologue comes a conversation between Pete and Mark, suggesting that their relationship in its turn is about to disintegrate; Mark now tells Pete that "You're an infection", and Pete replies:

> All I've got to do to destroy you is to leave you as you wish to be.

Here perhaps is the rarer dish anticipated by the dwarfs.[7]

Though the identity of the dwarfs is probably the real difficulty of the play, it is also true that Len's monologues on identity and perception demand far closer attention than anything in Pinter's stage plays. Like Edward in *A Slight Ache,* Len is obsessed with identity and perception. His difficulty in perceiving accurately objects outside himself is very much like that of Edward.

> The rooms we live in. . . open and shut. (*Pause.*) Can't you see? They change shape at their own will. I wouldn't grumble if only they would keep to some consistency. But they don't. And I can't tell the limits, the boundaries, which I've been led to believe are natural. I'm all for the natural behaviour of rooms, doors, staircases, the lot. But I can't rely on them. When, for example, I look through a train window, at night, and see the yellow lights, very clearly, I can see what they are, and I see that they're still. But they're only still because I'm moving. I know that they do move along with me, and when we go round a bend, they bump off. But I know they are still, just the same. They are, after all, stuck on poles which are rooted to the earth. So they must be still, in their own right, insofar as the earth itself is still, which of course it isn't. The point is, in a nutshell, that I can only appreciate such facts when I'm moving. When I'm still, nothing round me follows a natural course of conduct.

---

7. Pinter said in an interview: "It's a play about betrayal and mistrust. It does seem very confusing and obviously it can't be successful. But it was good for me to do." (*Theatre at Work,* ed. Charles Marowitz and Simon Trussler (London: Methuen, 1967), p. 101.

A speech by Len which is sometimes taken as being the crux of
The Dwarfs is actually an elaboration of Edward's final and agoni-
zed "Who are you?"

> The point is, who are you? Not why or how, or even what. I can
> see that, perhaps, clearly enough. But who are you?. . . Occasion-
> ally I believe I perceive a little of what you are but that's pure
> accident. Pure accident on both our parts, the perceived and the
> perceiver. It's nothing like an accident, it's deliberate, it's a joint
> pretence. We depend on these accidents, on these contrived ac-
> cidents, to continue. It's not important then that it's conspiracy
> or hallucination. What you are, or appear to be to me, or appear
> to be to you, changes so quickly, so horrifyingly, I certainly can't
> keep up with it and I'm damned sure you can't either. But who
> you are I can't even begin to recognize, and sometimes I recognize
> it so wholly, so forcibly, I can't look, and how can I be certain
> of what I see? You have no number. Where am I to look, where
> am I to look, what is there to locate, so as to have some surety,
> to have some rest from this whole bloody racket?

By way of contrast, in *The Homecoming* "this business of being
and non-being" is reduced cheerfully to Lenny's discussion with
his brother Teddy, a professional philosopher:

> LENNY. Well, for instance, take a table. Philosophically speaking.
>   What is it?
> TEDDY. A table.
> LENNY. Ah. You mean it's nothing else but a table. Well, some
>   people would envy your certainty, wouldn't they, Joey? For
>   instance, I've got a couple of friends of mine, we often sit round
>   the Ritz Bar having a few liqueurs, and they're always saying
>   things like that, you know, things like: Take a table, take it. all
>   right, I say, *take* it, *take* a table, but once you've taken it, what
>   you going to do with it? Once you've got hold of it, where you
>   are going to take it?

The shrewd suggestion of his father Max is:

> You'd probably sell it.

In *The Dwarfs* Pinter, contrary to his usual practice and even more
markedly than in *A Slight Ache,* is playing the philosopher, apparently with some seriousness; and it seems, from the history
of the play, that the roots of *The Dwarfs* may well go back to the
inspiration of Samuel Beckett.

Pinter has given consistent and generous acknowledgment of a debt to Beckett. In a B.B.C. interview in 1963, he told how, when he was about nineteen, and in Ireland, he picked up a copy of *Irish Writing* and read in it a piece called "Fragment from *Watt*":

> I looked at this and went cross-eyed and this was by Beckett, of course, this. . . this fragment. I didn't know he existed at all. I think he is the major writer of the day. It was a terrible business – a terrible business to read that fragment. Of course I went on to read Beckett a great deal.

Pinter was apparently referring to an "Extract from *Watt*" published in *Irish Writing* in 1951 (Pinter would actually have been about twenty-one), which might be described as a condensed version of Section III of Watt.[8] Beckett's novel had not at that time been published in full. From 1953 to 1957, Pinter was himself working on a novel. It was not published, but from "certain strains" of it, he later wrote *The Dwarfs*.[9] Pinter apparently made some drastic changes from the original, but the play is still veined with his early enthusiasm for Beckett.

Some of the affinities between the extract from *Watt* and *The Dwarfs* are general affinities, parallels which might equally be found if other works by Beckett and Pinter were compared, even though the two writers are fundamentally unlike. An obvious common bond is their sense of isolation and uncertainty. Most of Pinter's plays open with a hint of the isolation of the characters; even more emphatically stressed is the Pinter ending in isolation. This is also the pattern of the extract from *Watt*. As it opens we learn that Watt has been transferred to another pavilion, so that he and the narrator "consequently met, and conversed, less than formerly". It closes on a note of loneliness as Watt, after one of the rare meetings in the garden, returns to his pavilion, leaving the narrator "alone, with only my poor eyes to follow him, this last of many times to follow him. . ." Conversation between them is rare and governed by chance, for each is lured forth by different kinds of weather. They live surrounded by the unknown and uncertain, because "it was of course impossible to have any confidence in the meteorological information of our attendants". The resemblances here to Pinter's pervading uncertainties, the

---

8. *Irish Writing*, No. 17 (1951), pp. 11–16.
9. "Writing for Myself", *Twentieth Century*, CLXIX (February 1961), 172.

unequal attempts at communication between his characters, are unmistakable; perhaps for once Beckett is the more optimistic because his characters are at least momentarily "peers in peace", a state rarely enjoyed by Pinter's characters.

It is possible, however, to point to more specific resemblances between the "Extract from *Watt*" and *The Dwarfs*; in particular, some of Beckett's precise, objective passages of description are echoed in Pinter, typically made more colourful and emotional. Rats, for instance, appear in both extract and play. Beckett's rats "dwelt by the stream", and were the special friends of Watt and the narrator:

> They were long and black. We brought them such titbits from our ordinary as rinds of cheese, and morcels10 of gristle, and we brought them also birds' eggs, and frogs, and fledgelings. Sensible of these attentions, they would come flocking around us at our approach, with every sign of confidence and affection, and glide up our trouser-legs, and hang upon our breasts. And then we would sit down in the midst of them, and give them to eat, out of our hands, of a nice fat frog, or a baby thrush. Or seizing suddenly a plump young rat, resting in our bosom after its repast, we would feed it to its mother, or its father, or its brother, or its sister, or to some less fortunate relation.

Rats, equally unattractive, recur throughout *The Dwarfs*: the "rat corpse in the yellow grass" which Pete-the-gull finds as he "walks by the river" and tears to pieces ("with a snap the cloth of the rat's head tears"); the rats which must be pacified by Len when the dwarfs take a holiday, a picnic; the rat steak – "I tried all ways to please you" – which the dwarfs will not touch, but which, when Len can "no longer stand upright", they will bring out, "grimed then, green, varnished, rigid, and eat it as a victory dish". Is there also some memory or feeling of the Beckett passage in Pinter's recounting of the eating habits of his dwarfs, and the "scraps of cats' meat, pig bollocks, tin cans, bird brains, spare parts of all the little animals, a squelching, squealing carpet", that litter the yard?

Both Beckett and Pinter make what seems to be oblique allusion to the crucifixion. The narrator, describing Watt, says of him:

---

10. In the novel (London: John Calder, 1963) the spelling of this word is changed to the more conventional "morsels".

Then he turned, with the intention very likely of going back the
way he had come, and I saw his face, and the rest of his front. His
face was bloody, his hands also, and thorns were in his scalp.

The immediate association is with Christ, and the expanded version of the novel makes it quite clear that Beckett intended this.
In the novel, the next sentence, in parenthesis, reads:

(His resemblance, at that moment, to the Christ believed by Bosch,
then hanging in Trafalgar Square, was so striking, that I remarked
it.)

One might confidently believe that Len in *The Dwarfs* is identifying
himself with Christ, when he says:

LEN. . . . Here is my arrangement, and my kingdom. There are
no voices. They make no hole in my side. (*Whispering.*) They
make a hole, in my side.

and later:

LEN. . . . Both of you bastards, you've made a hole in my side, I
can't plug it! (*Pause.*) I've lost a kingdom.

The identification is not, on Pinter's part, a conscious one, and
he has said quite distinctly;

I have never intended any specific religious reference or been
conscious of using anything as a symbol for anything else.
"Mankind caught between the Old Testament God and the New
Testament God" makes no sense whatever to me in relation to
The Caretaker. The possible reference to Christ in the "they make
a hole in my side" quotation in *The Dwarfs* never occurred to
me. I certainly didn't mean it.

He adds, however:

I would remind you, on this question, that I live in the world like
everyone else and am part of history like everyone else.[11]

Finally, there is the complicated method of perambulation
adopted by Watt and the narrator in one of their rare moments of
communion:

Then I placed his hands, on my shoulders, his left hand on my
right shoulder, his right hand on my left shoulder. Then I placed

11. *Saturday Review,* L (8 April 1967), 97.

my hands, on his shoulders, on his left shoulder my right hand, on his right shoulder my left hand. Then I took a single step forward, with my left leg, and he took a single pace back, with his right leg (he could scarcely do otherwise.) Then I took a double pace forward, with my right leg, and he of course with his left leg a double pace back. And so we paced together between the fences, I forwards, he backwards, until we came to where they diverged again. And then turning, I turning, and he turning, we paced back the way we had come, I forwards, and he of course backwards, with our hands on our shoulders, as before. . . And so, up and down, we paced between the fences, together again after so long, and the sun shone bright upon us, and the wind blew wild about us.

Pinter's Mark and Pete, in their new alliance, walk back-to-back:

PETE. . . . We've been walking up the road back to back.
LEN. You've what? (*Pause.*) You've been walking up the road back back? (*Pause.*) What are you doing sitting on my bed? You're not supposed to sit on the bed, you're supposed to sit on the chairs!

Even if these unprovable "derivations" are accepted, one could not make too much of them; at best they demonstrate that Harold Pinter, like most young writers, was impressionable, influenced perhaps unconsciously by a style he admired, while his own was evolving.

The least pretentious, and probably the best, of Pinter's radio plays is *A Night Out*. It is a straightforward naturalistic drama, with enough plot to satisfy the most conventional drama-lover. Albert Stokes is a repressed and diffident young man, completely under the thumb of his domineering widowed mother. He asserts himself to the extent of going, against her wish, to an office party, given in honour of elderly Mr. Ryan who is retiring after a lifetime with the firm. While Albert and his colleagues are gathered round listening to a farewell speech to Mr. Ryan, one of the girls screams suddenly, explains that someone has touched her, taken "a liberty". Suspicion falls immediately on Albert (unjustly, the real culprit being Mr. Ryan), there is a scuffle between Albert and his overbearing, superior workmate, Gidney, and Albert leaves abruptly. At home he is greeted with a steady stream of reproachful nagging from his mother, largely on the theme (quite mythical) of his "mucking about with girls" and not leading "a clean life". Albert, pushed beyond endurance, picks up the clock, and turns to hurl it at his mother. In the next scene, he is taken home by a prostitute, an exaggeratedly "refined" female, who like his mother nags without stop. Clearly in his mind half-confusing her with his mother, Albert threatens to bash her also with a handy clock, reduces her to the abnegation of putting on his shoes. Two feet taller in self-confidence, Albert returns home, to find his mother, unharmed, waiting to forgive him. He slumps into despairing silence.

In many ways, *A Night Out* differs from other Pinter plays, and among the differences is the lack of what one might call typical Pinter uncertainty. Theme is clear-cut, the play simply a version of the tale of the silver cord; this is one of the few plays where one has a deep feeling of regret that the hero has failed to murder his mother, the fate ahead of him being obviously far more painful than mere hanging. Nor is there uncertainty about the characters, who are built along conventional lines, and in such a manner that we have the illusion that we know everything about them. The mother, for instance, explains abundantly her relationship with her son when she tells him (and us):

> One thing hurts me, Albert, and I'll tell you what it is. Not for years, not for years, have you come up to me and said, Mum, I love you, like you did when you were a little boy. You've never said it without me having to ask you. Not since before your father died.

(Perhaps Pinter has since felt he was too explicit; a later B.B.C. television broadcast of the play, on 13 February 1967, omitted "not since before your father died".) Normally Pinter is much more wary about dotting the i's and crossing the t's of his motivation and cause-and-effect; even in the more than usually explicit play *The Homecoming* we are left finally to wonder about the motives of the characters while we observe the fait accompli of their actions. In *A Night Out,* however, Albert, hysterically identifying the prostitute with his mother, is quite specific about the pressures that have brought about the whole horrible situation:

> ALBERT. . . . (*Viciously.*) Who do you think you are? You talk too much, you know that. You never stop talking. Just because you're a woman you think you can get away with it. (*Bending over her.*) You've made a mistake, this time. You've picked the wrong man.

He begins to grow in stature and excitement, passing the clock from hand to hand.

You're all the same, you see, you're all the same, you're just a dead weight round my neck. What makes you think... *(He begins to move around the room, at one point half-crouching, at another standing upright, as if exercising his body.)* What makes you think you can... tell me... yes... It's the same as this business about the light in Grandma's room. Always something. Always something *(To her.)* My ash? I'll put it where I like! You see this clock? Watch your step. Just watch your step!

Revealing that Gidney's taunts about his lack of success have added their mite. Albert adds:

I've got as many qualities at the next man.

If there is a touch of Pinter uncertainty in the play it comes in the final moments, when the Mother strokes Albert's hand and says:

You're good, you're not bad, you're a good boy... I know you are... you are, aren't you?

The hint of doubt lurking in the question may well communicate itself to the audience; there seems little prospect of a happy or normal future for Albert, but will he remain permanently crushed as he is now – or will some other provocation arise so that he does violence to his mother or to another woman? The mother's "you're a good boy" is rather like Meg's devoted "I think he's a good boy, although sometimes he's bad"; her "I know you are" seems an echo of Meg's constant "I know" in *The Birthday Party*, affirmation that she uses as a shield against doubt, but which in the end rouses only uncertainty in the mind of the audience.[12]

In performance, *A Night Out* is both moving and convincingly "real"; the mother comes alive as one of Pinter's choicest grotesque caricatures, overpowering and voracious, and the play conveys an overwhelming sense of Albert's frustration, his complete inability to break away from his prison. One of the memorable touches of the play is the way Pinter makes the Girl sound in fact exactly like the Mother; and avoids, with each of them, any effect of boredom for the audience as their nagging drones on, monotonous and implacable. *A Night Out* is not the kind of play to

12. See later, pp. 86 ff.

provoke lengthy discussion, but as a light radio play it is very good indeed. Coming as it does close to Pinter's more extreme experimental plays, *A Night Out* prompts the thought that perhaps Pinter may have written it to show that he could write a proper play if he felt like it.

Pinter fully appreciated the relative freedom offered by radio, and as he said, discussing *The Dwarfs*:

> From the point of view of content, I was able to go the whole hog and enjoy myself exploring to a degree which wouldn't be acceptable in any other medium.

In some respects, this sense of freedom was not wholly to the advantage of the plays. The B.B.C. Third Programme offered Pinter not only freedom to ignore popular taste, but more importantly popular comprehension, in *A Slight Ache* and *The Dwarfs* at least. *The Dwarfs* in particular is a difficult play, even for reading; the dialogue is tightly packed, and moving rapidly from thought to thought does not make sufficient concession to an audience struggling to follow and unable to turn back the page to re-read. At the end of Len's long speech, beginning "The point is, who are you?", a speech summarizing much of the thought of the play, the only point that the listener Mark has picked up is the simple personal one, "Pete thinks I'm a fool? (*Pause.*) Pete. . . Pete thinks that I'm a *fool?*" No doubt one should react to this only with awareness of Mark's self-centred nature, his implied interest in Pete, and his complete lack of understanding for Len; in fact, the audience may well feel nothing more than a flash of the sincerest fellow-feeling for Mark's bewilderment. Is the effort of following Pinter's difficult expression in *The Dwarfs,* and to a lesser extent *A Slight Ache,* worth while? One might suspect that in the end it is not, that the thought is very much simpler than the way it is expressed. Pinter is a playwright whose field is people; when he moves into the field of abstracts he can become pretentious rather than revealing. A contrast in this respect might be made with the earlier plays of Samuel Beckett, if not the later ones. Beckett experts can reveal endless labyrinths of complicated thought within the Beckett plays, but there is also a sufficiently simple framework, particularly in *Waiting for Godot*, to give the play meaning for a general audience and also enough "good theatre" to hold their interest; every minute something seems to be happening on stage in this play where "nothing happens, nobody comes, nobody goes, it's awful!"

Another weakness in *The Dwarfs* and *A Slight Ache* which might be blamed on Pinter's freedom to ignore audience appeal is the rather dull characterization. Radio theory has frequently suggested that radio is an ideal medium for the intimate exploration of character; for instance, the Hungarian playwright Miklós Gyárfas, writing in an introduction to his play, *Trials of Fidelity,* said:

> The radio play induces us to look inward... the radio leads us to the region of the soul.

Pinter shows in *A Night Out* that he is perfectly capable of creating vivid, living characters through dialogue alone, and so one cannot lay the blame for the shadowy beings of *A Slight Ache* and *The Dwarfs* on the radio medium per se, as being inimical to his style of character presentation. The point is rather that Pinter, in his absorption with philosophical problems, the private symbols of the characters, and the stream-of-consciousness technique he was exploring, simply allowed his characters to fade into mouthpieces of ideas, even though he *described* their appearance and essential character. This tendency is more marked in *The Dwarfs* than in *A Slight Ache,* where Edward and Flora retain some vestiges of personality, stereotyped though they may be.

A further question remains, however: how did Pinter adjust to the technical demands of radio, and how sensitively did he exploit its particular potentials? Harold Pinter has not shown himself an extremist in his use of the radio medium. His plays are not production pieces; there are no fireworks of radiophonic sound, and only occasionally naturalistic sound effects, such as "The door closes" (*A Slight Ache*) or "The sound of a recorder being played. The sound is fragmentary." (*The Dwarfs*). Pinter shows none of the instinct to exploit sound in the way he exploited the visual effects of the stage right from the beginning. *The Dwarfs* is particularly short on sound effects, the only background sounds being a recorder, a door slamming, a toasting fork falling to the hearth, steps on a road, and "hospital sounds". *The Dwarfs* has a particular weakness of radio technique, not found in the other radio plays, in its cross-fades. Scene changes are quite legitimately marked by silence rather than by extraneous sounds such as music, but the author fails sometimes to make the elementary

concession to his listeners of letting it be clear that the scene
has indeed changed. An example occurs early in the play. *The
Dwarfs* begins with a conversation between Len and Pete, Mark
arrives home off-mike (indicated by Pete's "Ssshh! That's him",
and a door slamming), and there follows: "Voices of greeting,
fading". After a moment's silence, Len launches into his first
interior monologue. At the end of it comes another silence, and
then Len *begins speaking again* – this time not to himself but to
Mark. At this early stage we are not yet accustomed to the alterna-
tion of monologue and dialogue, and the change over is unneces-
sarily confusing. The situation would have been clearer if, very
simply, Mark had been allowed the first line in the conversation
with Len. Worse however is to follow. For once, the conversation
between Len and Mark is not followed by a monologue from Len,
as mostly happens, but by a conversation between Len and Pete.
Again, and very confusingly, Len has the last word in the conversation with Mark, and the first word in the conversation with
Pete.

> LEN. But when the time comes, you see, what I shall do is place
> the red hot burning coal in my own mouth.
>
> *Silence.*
>
> I've got some beigels.

Presumably a producer would fade out "in my own mouth" and
fade in "I've got some beigels", even though this is not indicated,
but the human ear is exceedingly fallible, and cross-fades, unless
they are long enough to throw away a number of words (more than
can be spared here), are not in themselves a completely reliable
way of marking change of scene. The clumsiness of technique
here imposes an extra strain on the listener, who may in the case
of *The Dwarfs* be presumed to be already working hard enough.
    However, even if Pinter did not show any inclination to exploit
the non-verbal sound potentials of radio, he did respond immediately and sensitively to the three qualities which are funda-
mental to radio drama: that is, intimacy, flexibility, and the
pre-eminence of the word.
    The sudden increased flexibility of setting in Pinter's radio
plays, so that they move at will outside the room, has already been
mentioned, but the possible flexibility of radio as a medium for

drama goes beyond the freedom to move one's setting at will, even, if one cares to, from the bottom of a coal mine to the valleys of the moon; the flexibility of radio means more than this, and is closely linked with the second attribute of radio drama, its intimacy. Though it is a long time since radio drama was produced simply by taking microphones into the theatre, so that the listening audience could hear the voices, thumps, and bangs of a current stage success, many modern radio writers still follow very much the pattern of stage drama, even though they may allow themselves the liberty of changing the setting more frequently than is practical on the stage. *A Night Out* belongs to this type of radio play; for publication, it has been divided into acts and scenes, meaningless in radio, and it not only transferred readily to the television medium, but is also most effective, and not difficult to mount, in the theatre. However, the radio play which exploits to the hilt the special qualities belonging to radio alone is often closer to narrative form than to the stage play; it may even suggest the modern version of the tale told round the camp fire. Many of the best radio plays have in fact taken the form of narration interspersed with dialogue: Dylan Thomas's *Under Milkwood,* for example, and the play by the Australian poet Douglas Stewart, *The Fire on the Snow. The Dwarfs* comes very close to this basically narrative form. Len is certainly not narrating to us, the audience, but he does allow us to hear his thoughts; the result is a kind of stream-of-consciousness technique, not normally equated with stage drama, but today more and more frequently exploited by radio. (Another example is the radio version of Ingmar Bergman's *The City*.) It is a technique which at best can produce a painful intimacy, an overwhelming sense of one's being inside the mind of the character. Of all Pinter's radio plays, *The Dwarfs* would be the most difficult to adapt to any other medium, though it has been given stage performance. *A Slight Ache* does not cast quite so far adrift from the conventional stage form as does *The Dwarfs,* but again it does at times achieve a piercing sense of intimacy, as Edward speaks out his thoughts: the silence of the unseen Matchseller contributes to the impression that he is speaking to us alone.

Again, however, the effect of Pinter's immersion in radio technique is not wholly to the advantage of the play. A close look at *A Slight Ache,* and to an even greater extent *The Dwarfs,* suggests how important, in holding audience attention, are the moments of theatrical (often visual) shock in Pinter's stage plays. Tending towards the narrative form in these two radio plays, he has dispensed with theatrical shocks, and found nothing equally effective to replace them. *A Slight Ache* has the tension of our realizing that Edward is slowly destroying himself, but in *The Dwarfs* the "plot" (the expulsion of Len from the triangle) is too well hidden to provide much relief from the tight and difficult dialogue. At times, the play comes close to monotony.

What, finally, of Pinter's response to the third attribute of radio drama, the responsibility it lays on words, as a substitute for vision? This responsibility is of course considerable, words (except in purely radiophonic drama) normally doing most of the work in a radio play; even where sound effects are used more extensively than in Pinter's plays, they usually need to be reinforced or explained by dialogue, to compensate for the fallibility of the human ear which finds it difficult to distinguish whether a lightly tapping sound on radio is a close-up of a pencil being knocked on a desk or a tree being chopped down a quarter of a mile away. It is no accident that many of the best radio playwrights have been poets, and poets very much given to vivid imagery; memories of a good radio play (even, one might suggest, of Tom Stoppard's *Albert's Bridge*) are surprisingly often visual. Two of Pinter's radio plays, *A Slight Ache* and *The Dwarfs,* are verbally visual in a way that his stage plays are not; in particular, *A Slight Ache* shows most markedly this ability to create a scene, simply through hints in the dialogue.

The most vivid impression of the setting of *A Slight Ache* is the garden, "suggested at the back of the stage" in the theatre-adaptation. From the opening line of the play when Flora asks "Have you noticed the honeysuckle this morning?" we are hardly allowed to forget it. It is used to suggest character; Edward, though aware of the names of the plants in his garden, cannot attach the right name to to right plant, while Flora obviously knows her garden intimately. Because he works in the garden, we learn that Edward needs a canopy to shade him from the sun and the wind. It is a garden at the height of summer, and Flora states four times in the course of the play that it is the longest day of the year. All the flowers mentioned, except japonica, are creeping vines, with a tendency to cover and strangle with their sweetness: honeysuckle, convolvulus, clematis. In this sweet-scented garden, by the gate where the Matchseller stands, there are nettles. Flora first refers to them as she guides the Matchseller in:

May I take your arm? There's a good deal of *nettle* inside the gate.

The italics are Pinter's, the only ones to occur in the dialogue of the play, so it is probably not far-fetched to suggest that he meant the word to have emphasis. Edward mentions the nettles again when he is close to his breaking-point, with an obvious association of ideas:

... I was ready for my excursions to the cliff, down the path to the back gate, through the long grass, no need to watch for nettles, my progress was fluent, after my long struggling against all kinds of usurpers, disreputables, lists, literally lists, of people anxious to do me down, and my reputation down, my command was established...

In the room with the view of the garden, a wasp is drowned in the sticky sweetness of the marmalade jar. The heroine, whose name is Flora, presumably a name intended to have associations, seems to be identified with the garden; there is a cloying sweetness about her:

FLORA. Oh, Weddie. Beddie-weddie...
EDWARD. Do not call me that!

At the risk of being painfully obvious, one might suggest that the nettle shows through at the end. In the closing scene of the play, Flora leads the Matchseller from Edward's study (Edward seems to be identified with the study, where he can close the windows, as Flora is identified with the garden) out into the garden, telling him:

I want to show you my garden, your garden. You must see my japonica, my convolvulus... my honeysuckle, my clematis.

With significant change of tense from her usual statement that it is the longest day of the year, she adds:

The summer is coming.

Above all, the constant references to the summer garden help to give a sense of overpowering heat and sweetness, permeating the play.

Even beyond this use of the garden setting, *A Slight Ache* is a visual play. Edward's and Flora's memories of what might be called the romantic interests of their youth are colourful; Edward remembers that the squire's daughter had red hair, while the poacher who raped Flora grew a red beard. Edward's revelation of his thoughts towards the end of the play comes out largely in visual images, conveying his meaning in indirect allusion; these speeches come closest to the nonsensical speeches of menace in *The Birthday Party* and *The Caretaker*. Although, as suggested, the setting of *The Dwarfs* is not really important, nevertheless the moments of the play that remain in the mind tend, once again, to be visual: the descriptions of Pete, of Mark, of the dwarfs, of the rooms that "change shape at their own will", of the yellow lights seen from the train window that "bump off" when the train goes round a bend. The dialogue of *A Night Out* is quite different; one reason why it transferred so successfully to television is that it is not loaded with visual imagery, ran no risk of seeming over-written in the intensely pictorial medium of T.V. The dialogue of *A Night Out* is perhaps the least mannered of any Pinter play to date; examined closely, it exhibits, in each character, the familiar Pinter authenticity, down to the "oh" with which the yes-man Mr. Horne prefaces each remark addressed to his employer.

3 the caretaker and "failure of communication"

It is not easy to suggest in a few words the difference between Pinter's second full-length stage play, *The Caretaker,* and the comedies of menace. One might perhaps describe it as a mixture of naturalism and Pinter grotesquerie, a kind of cross between *The Birthday Party* and *A Night Out. The Caretaker* is a more austere play than *The Birthday Party,* and more sombre; it moves us for different reasons. There is an element of the thriller in the way *The Birthday Party* rouses pity and terror in its audiences, far less of this in *The Caretaker.* Our pity and terror spring rather from the spectacle of man inflicting hurt upon man, a sight that is moving with the pain of recognition rather than blind apprehension. This is not of course to say that the theatrical devices for keeping us nervously alert in our seats have disappeared altogether.

Aston, "a man in his early thirties", slowly recovering it seems from shock treatment in a mental asylum, still uncertain and slow-thinking, gives shelter to Davies, an old vagrant who has just lost his job in a café after being involved in a brawl. Aston tentatively offers friendship to Davies, who regards him as some kind of nut and determines to curry favour instead with Aston's younger,

more powerful and enigmatic brother Mick; Davies hopes to
dislodge Aston from his room and take over himself as caretaker.
Mick, shrewd and ruthless, encourages Davies in his schemes sufficiently for him to become over-confident and show his hand
to Aston. Then both brothers reject the old man, and the play
ends with his frantic pleas for another chance finally trailing into
silence when Aston, now implacable, tells him to get out.

At first sight, any audience could well believe that it was in for
yet another comedy of menace, dominated by an unexplained and
terrifying agent. When the curtain rises, we see a man standing
alone on stage, wearing the leather jacket one tends to associate
with motor-bikes, violence, and Marlon Brando films. Voices
are heard off-stage, the voices of Aston and Davies approaching,
and the leather-jacketed man slips silently away. Our suspicions
are instantly aroused. What danger threatens the unsuspecting
inhabitants of the room? This initial uncertainly generated in the
audience has a very useful practical value, gripping the attention
of the audience and holding it through a scene where very little
actually happens, and where the slowly unwinding conversation
between Aston and Davies, setting background and giving necessary information, might without our apprehension that something
evil or dangerous is waiting in the wings seem too quiet and
subdued to hold our interest. The man in the leather jacket has
suggested danger, and the tension generated by his unexplained
presence hovers over the scene and explodes into terror at the
end of it, when he reappears while Davies, alone, is poking about
among Aston's possessions; forcing the old man to his knees
until he screams with pain, the mysterious figure asks "What's
the game?" Act II takes up the situation moments later, as the
menace-figure questions Davies, his probing, relentlessly reiterated
questions interspersed with illogical biographies about a series
of colourful and unlikely people such as his uncle's brother who
had a penchant for nuts, nothing else but a penchant, and carried
his fiddle on his back like a papoose. It is something like the
interrogation and wooing scenes of *The Birthday Party*. Then
Aston returns, takes the presence of the violent stranger quite
casually, and we see that they are on good terms, though they
say little to each other. Later, Aston explains to Davies that the
tormentor was his brother Mick. The mystery is over. Mick is
no inexplicable agent of menace, possibly supernatural; he is a

ruthless human being using very effective terrorization techniques. This moment of casual explanation marks the essential difference between *The Caretaker* and the comedies of menace which preceded it. In *The Caretaker* there is no longer unexplained mystery, and no actions which cannot be accounted for in terms of familiar human motive. No longer is the menace a mysterious agent from without, or even a passive catalyst before whom the hero destroys himself; now Pinter sees the inhabitants of the room menacing the authority of each other, in their search for personal security. This pattern was foreshadowed by *The Dwarfs*, and perhaps has its roots in Pinter's concept, from the beginning, of the vulnerability of the agent of menace himself.

The room, in spite of the shift of emphasis from mystery to motivation, retains its familiar position as keystone of the play – Pinter continues to exploit his room setting to the full, both thematically and theatrically. Mick, Aston, and Davies menace the security of each other because they come into conflict over possession of the room. The one who actually owns the room does not live in it, or at least not continuously: Mick, who has "deeds to prove it". The fact that he does not live there does not make him any less possessive about the room; he constantly asserts ownership. Why is the room so valuable to him? Throughout the play Mick lures us with his dreams of it when it has been re-furnished, with mahogany and rosewood furniture and "deep azure-blue carpet, unglazed blue and white curtains, a bedspread with a pattern of small blue roses on a white ground, dressing-table with a lift-up top containing a plastic tray, table lamp of white raffia", and so on. Then, in his show-down with Davies, he tells him and us:

> I'm not worried about this house. I'm not interested. My brother can worry about it. He can do it up, he can decorate it, he can do what he likes with it. I'm not bothered. I thought I was doing him a favour, letting him live here.

Is Mick a dreamer, the re-furnished flat being his equivalent of Aston's shed and Davies' journey to Sidcup? Or is his vision simply a practical therapy for the restoration of his brother, his long flights of description of it artillery in his word-warfare against Davies? Mick's possessiveness is matched by the would-be possessiveness of Davies, who has no rights in the room at all but struggles for undivided possession. For Davies, the vagrant, the have-not, the room represents security, a place to live, a place where "you'd be well out of the draught. . .", and perhaps life itself. Aston, the permanent inhabitant, is the only one willing (in the beginning at least) to share the room; to him also it presumably represents security, a refuge from the world, and a place where he can store his junk, mend the toaster, plan a shed.

If the attitude of the characters to the room itself tells us a great deal about them, their comments on the furnishings with which it is crowded are also revealing. As in the earlier Pinter stage plays, the room in which *The Caretaker* is set is a shabby, untidy place; but while the earlier rooms were emphatically credible, perhaps familiar places, this one is grotesque, almost bizarre. It is not a fantasy room; one feels that it probably exists many times over in the attics of London, but piled with odd junk ranging from the plaster Buddha on the unconnected gas stove to the bucket hanging from the ceiling, it has some of the stagey unreality of a secondhand dealer's yard. In previous plays the credibility of the room had balanced and underlined the bizarre happenings on the stage; now comparatively naturalistic characters and events move against a bizarre though not impossibly unreal setting. The black and white striped china of *The Dumb Waiter* gave a sense of homely familiarity; in *The Caretaker* the electrolux becomes an instrument of terror in the darkened room.

Aston, who collected the rubbish, "thought it might come in handy"; it is part of his vague dream of the future, along with the shed he will one day build. Perhaps it is also an attempt to shore up his life against insecurity through possessions. Davies is impressed by the collection. "You got a good bit of stuff here" is his verdict, and he immediately translates it into terms of hard cash:

> Must be worth a few bob, this. . . put it all together.

Davies' speeches have a habit of revealing something different from what the speaker intended to convey, and ignorance and an eye for hard cash show through this comment (plus the desire to appear at all times the expert) rather than an informed judgment on the monetary value of the junk. Mick makes the only really practical and realistic assessment of it, but fails to take into account the part it plays in Aston's dreams, as he tells Davies:

All this old junk here, it's no good to anyone. It's just a lot of old iron, that's all. Clobber. You couldn't make a home out of this. It's junk. He could never sell it, either, he wouldn't get tuppence for it.

One may even read a kind of symbolism into the way the characters handle various objects of furniture. The gas stove is perfectly harmless and not even connected to the main, but it is feared by Davies because he does not understand it. He is afraid that he might accidentally nudge one of the taps while he is asleep; equally he fears the radiator. Mick picks up the statue of the Buddha, traditionally inscrutable, and smashes it in the one moment in the play when his normally inscrutable self-control breaks, and he speaks out passionately and directly his own feelings about the situation to Davies:

THAT'S WHAT I WANT!

Perhaps Aston's constant fiddling with the toaster cord suggests a desire to make and mend, as well of course as giving an actor who spends a great part of his time quietly listening something to do with his hands.

In one sense, the play also retains the familiar invader from without in the person of Davies, coming into the room and quickly showing intent to harm the inhabitant. Certainly Mick sees him from the beginning as an intruder, tells him:

You come busting into a private house, laying your hands on anything you can lay your hands on. Don't overstep the mark, son.

But in this economical play each character has two roles, both victim and menace, and, as suggested, their motives are quite explicable in familiar human terms. Aston is threatened by Davies, and Mick may also regard Davies as a threat, not only to the brother whom he protects, but to his own close if not particularly vocal relationship with Aston. Mick shows a surprising flash of jealousy in the scene where Aston brings home a bag of clothes for Davies. Mick will not allow Davies to take the bag till Aston has handed it first to Mick himself. Then he passes it to Davies. Equally, and more successfully, the brothers threaten the new-found security of Davies. Mick manipulates his ruin, and Aston speaks the fatal words of rejection at the end of the play, brutally

apt in the desperate stream of Davies's pleading for another
chance –

You make too much noise.

A natural result of this swing from mystification to psychological
realism is that it is more important in *The Caretaker* than in the
comedies of menace for the characters to be convincing and
worthy of interest; and Pinter meets the challenge. He does not
of course change his technique of character presentation; he still
refuses to tell all, he caricatures slightly, with deft repeated strokes.
Davies in particular is a triumph, the kind of character who
almost seems to have a life apart from the play, and who, to a
degree unusual for Pinter, demands of the audience the kind of
divided reaction that normally makes us say a character is "complex". One is torn continually between pity and dislike; in
performance, of course, an actor can emphasize one aspect of him
at the expense of another. Davies is one of Pinter's greedy, overpowering characters, related, even though distantly, to the
Mother in *A Night Out,* Max in *The Homecoming,* and even perhaps Goldberg in *The Birthday Party.* At the same time he is
a pitiful, homeless old man, losing his Eden through his own
greed and stupidity. His development from gratitude to arrogance
and treachery, then back to a plea for pity, is made to seem
completely inevitable, the predictable behaviour of one who
combines suspicion, evasiveness, greed, misplaced trust, big talk,
and personal cowardice. The firmness of Pinter's grasp on the
character shows in one very subtle touch at the beginning of the
play, a use of words so subtle that no theatre audience could be
expected to notice it consciously, but suggesting how completely
Pinter visualizes the beings of his imagination: that is, Davies'
use of the word "have". Greed is one of the strongest forces in
Davies; it is demonstrated in the action of the play, as he first takes
with gratitude whatever Aston offers – shelter, a seat, a bit of
tobacco – then finally demands the whole room. Although in the
opening scene we have not yet had time to observe the greed of
the man in significant action, nevertheless, in his first eight
speeches (all quite short), Davies uses the word "have", in the
possessive sense, eight times! After this, the incidence of the
possessive "have" in Davies' speech falls away, though more
concrete demonstrations of his acquisitiveness mount. Pinter

may have repeated these words of possession unconsciously, they may have risen naturally out of his vision of Davies' insatiable greed; or he may have written them with considered judgment to help shape our early vision of Davies, unawares. More obvious, and more effective dramatically, is the author's understanding of what would be important to a man in Davies' position: shoes, a place without draughts, a piece of soap. Realistic too are his constant demands for respect, hand in hand with the implications of past strength, no longer able to assert itself. It is not surprising that in painting Davies, Pinter apparently had a real-life tramp in mind, even though he drew on him only for occasional phrases.[1]

It would be easy to make too much of this change in Pinter's writing; to discuss *The Caretaker* solely in terms of the way psychological realism has dislodged the supernatural would be flagrant misplacement of emphasis, and could suggest a far more radical change in Pinter's work than has actually taken place. After all, vivid if not profound characterization has always been one of the best features of Pinter's plays; and for all the increasing realism of *The Caretaker,* its subject – man's uncertain footing in his universe – is unchanged.

Theatrical shock devices, some familiar from earlier plays, keep the audience in the first two acts in a state of nervous alertness: Mick's interrogation of Davies at the beginning of Act II, reminiscent of the interrogation of Stanley by Goldberg and McCann in *The Birthday Party*; the scene where the stage is plunged in darkness while Mick terrorizes Davies with the electrolux, reminding us of the game of blind man's buff in a suddenly darkened room in *The Birthday Party*; and, already discussed, the unexplained and therefore sinister presence of Mick at the beginning of the play. These theatrical devices reinforce the deep uncertainty generated by the characters.

Mick, Aston, and Davies are wary and suspicious as jungle animals, not only of each other but of the universe at large. On the face of things it might seem absurd to suggest that Mick, the self-concealing, ruthless manipulator of events, is insecure, but his very ruthlessness and instant suspicion of Davies suggest a hard school where he has learnt that such savagery is necessary

---

1. Peter Lewis, "Harold Pinter: Fascinated by Unsatisfactory People", *Time and Tide*, XLIII (21 June 1962), 17.

for survival. Aston is gentler. One feels that his is the mildness of the deeply hurt – he tells Davies how he once talked too much of his visions, because he thought people understood; and he talks of the one day he was taken away –

> But I don't talk to people now. I steer clear of places like the cafe. I never go into them now. I don't talk to anyone. . . like that.

In spite of his hard-learned caution, Aston still apparently feels the need to give and to confide, as his early generosity to Davies shows, and his slow development from monosyllabic reticence to a long speech about the treatment given him in the asylum. Aston seems very vulnerable, and our sympathy for him is heightened by the automatic pity one tends to feel for the maimed. There is both irony and sound psychology in the fact that Davies, the menacing and graspingly hungry invader of the room, is himself the most insecure of the characters. His terrifying insecurity is established in the opening moments of the play. He is a tramp, he is homeless, and no longer either young or strong:

> I remember the days when I was as handy as any of them. They didn't take any liberties with me. But I haven't been so well lately. I've had a few attacks.

Whatever the truth of the matter, he at least feels himself to be at the mercy of all the Greeks, Poles, and Blacks who take the seats in the tea-break at the café where he worked, the Scotch git who tells him to empty buckets (though according to Davies this is not his job) and apparently intends to beat him up, the mysterious person(s) who pinched his tobacco on the Great West Road, and even the priest at the monastery at Luton who told him to have a meal and then "piss off out of it". Many of Pinter's characters are suspicious of foreigners (even Mick enquires of Davies "You a foreigner?"), but Davies is obsessed with foreigners, aliens, who are of course doubly suspect if they are also "Blacks". Like the gas stove and the radiator, they represent the unknown. Davies is invariably non-committal about his past; whatever it is, he will not deliver himself into the hands of a potential enemy by speaking of it. Equally suspicious and insecure is his reaction to any unexpected proposition for future or present, always a cautious evasion, to give himself time to think it over, whether it is an invitation by Aston to stay a while with him, or the offer of a job as caretaker, first by Aston then by Mick. To the first offer, of shelter, he says:

> Oh, I don't know about that.

To Aston's suggestion that he be caretaker:

> Well, I... I never done caretaking before, you know... I mean to say... I never... what I mean to say is... I never been a caretaker before

and

> Well, I reckon... Well, I'd have to know... you know...

When Mick offers him a job as caretaker, Davies replies with similar caution:

> Well now... wait a minute... I... I ain't never done no caretaking before, you know.

Again ironically, though Davies himself is the alien, the invader of the room, he is himself the one who expresses fear of invasion from without. He is not quite sure whether or not he ought, in his capacity as caretaker, to answer queries at the front door:

> I mean, you don't know what might come up them front steps, do you? I got to be a bit careful.

A particular speech habit of the characters, familiar also in real life, helps in a minor key to suggest the unknown quality of the world surrounding Aston, Mick, and Davies, a world populated with shadowy, faceless figures: that is, the unidentified "they". "They" in real life leave the parks littered with rubbish, misrule the country, and fail students in examinations. It is in this general sense that Mick asks Davies:

> What did they teach you?

and Davies explains why he should be in demand to work in the café:

> What they want to do, they're trying to do away with these foreigners, you see, in catering. They want an Englishman to pour their tea, that's what they want, that's what they're crying out for.

Generally in Pinter, however, "they" have sinister overtones. "They" are not of course found only in *The Caretaker*; they appear also, for instance, in *The Birthday Party,* with deliberate terrifying ambiguity in Stanley's story to Meg of "them", who are coming with a van and wheelbarrow, looking for someone. "They" with slightly sinister overtones figure in the dialogue of both Aston and Davies; not of Mick. "They" did not take liberties with Davies when he was young and strong, but in later years they haven't stamped his card, and will punish him if they find out his real identity:

> DAVIES. . . . That's not my real name, they'd find out, they'd have me in the nick. Four stamps. I haven't paid out pennies, I've paid out pounds, not pennies. There's been other stamps, plenty, but they haven't put them on, the nigs, I never had enough time to go into it.
>
> ASTON. They should have stamped your card.

"They" might even take Davies unawares if in his capacity as caretaker he answered the front door bell:

> They might be there after my card, I mean look at it, here I am, I only got four stamps, on this card, here it is, look, four stamps, that's all I got, I ain't got any more, they'd have me in, that's what they'd do, I wouldn't stand a chance.

On the other hand, towards the end of the play "they" apparently stand euphemistically for Mick, as Davies explains to Aston:

> I've been offered a good job. Man offered it to me, he's . . . he's got plenty of ideas. He's got a bit of a future. But they want my papers, you see, they want my references.

"They" appear also in Aston's long speech about his treatment in the asylum. We are left in no real doubt about who "they" are (actually one usually knows who Davies' "they" are also); in Aston's speech, "they" are first the men he talked to without sufficiently guarding his speech, and then the doctors and attendants in the hospital who treated him. But as with Davies' "they", the fact that these people are referred to impersonally de-humanizes them; we see them not as factory workers or doctors but as shadowy figures feared by Aston, existing only to inflict pain.

> ASTON. . . . They were all. . . a good bit older than me. But they used to listen. I thought. . . they understood what I said. I mean I used to talk to them. I talked too much. That was my mistake. The same in the factory. Standing there, or in the breaks, I used to. . . talk about things.

Later:

ASTON. . . . Then one day they took me to a hospital, right outside
London. They. . . got me there. I didn't want to go. Anyway. . .
I tried to get out, quite a few times. But. . . it wasn't very easy.
They asked me questions, in there. Got me in and asked me
all sorts of questions. Well, I told them. . . when they wanted
to know. . . what my thoughts were.

And so on, till Aston is finally cornered by "them" and "this chief"
puts the pincers on his skull. After this final moment of horror,
"they" do not appear again in Aston's speech. "They" belong to
the terrifying shadows of the struggle, not to the comparative
peace of resignation.

One cannot talk of Pinter's plays, and *The Caretaker* in
particular, without bringing into the discussion, sooner or later,
what Pinter himself has called "that tired, grimy phrase: 'Failure
of communication'". Isolation is the common fate of Pinter
characters; it is part of the insecurity of their world that they
should be alone. Usually Pinter devotes the opening moments of
his plays to establishing lack of communication between his
characters, not in this early stage with any sense of menace, but
lightly, almost humorously; and, with his habit of repeating
devices that work, he has in four of his five stage plays to date used
exactly the same opening situation to suggest at least temporary
non-communication between the characters: that is, the situation
where one character is trying to talk to another who is absorbed in
a newspaper or book, a state which we all know is one of the
most effective barriers to communication devised by man. In
The Room, Rose chatters in a long monologue while Bert, without
a word, eats, and reads the magazine propped up in front of him.
At the beginning of *The Dumb Waiter*, Ben is also reading his
newspaper, though he does occasionally lower it to watch Gus
moving restlessly round the room, and even reads aloud to him
occasional anecdotes. He takes little notice, behind his paper,
when Gus tries to ask him questions, though he pays more attention later in the play. In the opening scenes of *The Birthday Party*,
Petey, like Bert, is trying to read while he eats, but unlike Bert he
does make some sort of response, however monosyllabic, to his
wife's chatter, and gives her bits of social gossip from his newspaper. *The Homecoming* opens with Max furiously trying to break
through Lenny's concentration as he too sits reading a newspaper.

The Caretaker is in fact the exception to this rule. Although failure of communication is to be a very important aspect of it, the play opens with what is clearly an attempt at communication between two human beings, imperfect though this may be. Aston has just saved Davies from being beaten up, and in some way seems to be drawn to him; his attitude is a generous one, even if he is offering only a seat, a piece of tobacco. Davies, shaken by his experience, is still grateful and prepared to say: "That's kind of you, mister."

Pinter, as has been many times reported, differs from the majority of Absurdists (and of course other non-Absurd writers past and present) who feel that man is unable to communicate, however much he may desire to do so; Pinter declares that on the contrary man avoids communication whenever possible. Martin Esslin quotes a statement made by Pinter in an interview with Kenneth Tynan:

> "I feel", he once said, "that instead of any inability to communicate there is deliberate evasion of communication. Communication itself between people is so frightening that rather than do that there is continual cross-talk, a continual talking about other things, rather than what is at the root of their relationship."[2]

In a later interview, he further stressed the idea that communication does actually take place, unless we can manage to keep it at bay by talking about something else, by constant evasion.

> I think that we communicate only too well, in our silence, in what is unsaid, and that what takes place is continual evasion, desperate rearguard attempts to keep ourselves to ourselves. Communication is too alarming. To disclose to others the poverty within us is too fearsome a possibility.[3]

In this evasion of communication, language plays its part, to help conceal rather than reveal:

> Language. . . is a highly ambiguous commerce. So often, below words spoken, is the thing known and unspoken. . . There are two silences. One when no word is spoken. The other when perhaps a torrent of language is being employed. This speech is

---

speaking of a language locked beneath it. That is its continual reference. The speech we hear is an indication of that we don't hear. It is a necessary avoidance, a violent, sly, anguished or mocking smoke-screen which keeps the other in its place. When true silence falls we are still left with echo but are nearer nakedness. One way of looking at speech is to say it is a constant stratagem to cover nakedness.[4]

Any Pinter play could serve to document these comments, any of the dozen evasive, non-committal characters, from Mr. Kidd in *The Room* to Davies himself. Often fear is clearly visible behind their unwillingness to communicate, though sometimes, as with the boorish Bert in *The Room*, one would be delving deep to find fear as the motive. More exciting, more complex, and more typically Pinter, are the moments – and there are many of them – where communication does take place, real and intense communication, though never rising from the surface meanings of the words spoken, and often, as Pinter suggests, when the characters are employing a torrent of language to ward off open communication. Stanley understands perfectly the implied menace of Goldberg and McCann in *The Birthday Party,* though on the surface their interrogation does not seem to contain sufficient threat to reduce him to abject pulp, as it actually does. Davies also understands the terrifying illogicality of Mick's long reminiscences about his uncle's brother who was always on the move and had a penchant for nuts, nothing else but a penchant, and the bloke he once knew in Shoreditch who actually lived in Aldgate; as Mick begins the third biography ("You know, you remind me of a bloke I bumped into once, just the other side of the Guildford by-pass – "), Davies has had enough, he cracks and answers Mick's unspoken question, tells him "I was brought here! I was brought here!" Similarly, when towards the end of the play Mick accuses Davies of masquerading as an interior decorator ("You wouldn't be able to decorate out a table in afromosia teak veneer, an armchair in oatmeal tweed and a beech frame settee with a woven sea-grass seat?... You're a bloody impostor, mate!"), Mick knows, and Davies knows, that Mick never did think Davies was an interior decorator, but below the words, unspoken, Mick is rejecting Davies, telling him to get out.

---

4. *Ibid.*

The Dumb Waiter, balancing on tensions only obliquely expressed in words, is probably Pinter's most sustained example
of speech that is "a necessary avoidance, a violent, sly, anguished
or mocking smoke-screen". One of the funniest, and only on
second thoughts alarming, scenes in the play is the gas-kettle
passage, where Ben and Gus come to blows over whether it is
more correct to say "light the kettle" or "light the gas". In fact,
when they are not thinking of what they are saying, each man
uses unconsciously the term for which he criticizes the other.
Before the quarrel begins, Gus remarks:

> I can light the kettle now.

However, seconds later, presumably irritated by Ben slapping his
hand down when he thoughtfully probes his ear with a match,
Gus criticizes Ben for saying exactly the same thing, light the
kettle, and corrects it to:

> You mean the gas.

The battle is on, Ben asserts with great determination:

> I have never in all my life heard anyone say put on the kettle

and then of course when the quarrel subsides, himself says wearily:

> Put on the bloody kettle, for Christ's sake.

They both register what has been said, but with commendable
diplomacy Gus retreats to a neutral position and reports that the
stove is going. In a stage performance, the dialogue and action
tend to move too quickly for the audience to be aware that both
men use both forms, thus making it clear that neither of them
really cares for such linguistic subtleties; but even if one does not
realize this, it is clear enough that Gus and Ben in their pedantic
argument are simply letting off steam about the threat hanging
over Gus which they are not willing to discuss. A less amusing
scene of communication without words occurs at the end of the
play, where Ben looks at his newspaper, exclaims at what is
there without actually reading it aloud, and Gus, almost inaudible,
comments as if Ben were still telling him what was written.
Obliquely this passage suggests the hopelessness of Gus's position,
and how completely he has given up the fight against whatever
awaits him.

Pinter does not suggest, however, that his evasive, self-protective characters are so controlled and self-sufficient that they never feel the need to communicate directly, to speak out. As Pinter says in "Pinter Between the Lines":

> I'm not suggesting that no character in a play can ever say what he in fact means. Not at all. I have found that there invariably does come a moment when this happens, when he says something, perhaps, which he has never said before. And where this happens, what he says is irrevocable, and can never be taken back.

Sometimes such characters speak out in a brief outburst, as Mick does in his impassioned "Anyone would think this house was all I got to worry about" speech in Act III of *The Caretaker*; sometimes they make a more prolonged effort, as does Edward in the lengthy self-revelations of *A Slight Ache*. However, when the Pinter character does step so far outside himself as to seek for sympathetic understanding, the general rule is that he will fail to get it. Edward is finally rejected by the Matchseller, who apparently laughs at him. Len in *The Dwarfs* pours out in a long speech the problems that are oppressing him, but all that Mark hears and registers is a reference to himself:

> Pete thinks you're a fool.

When Teddy in *The Homecoming* states his creed of objectivity ("It's a question of how far you can operate on things and not in things. . . I won't be lost in it"), his speech is followed by a quick blackout, and his family gives no sign of having heard him.

Of all Pinter's plays, however, *The Caretaker* comes closest to being specifically about an attempt at communication which fails. The pattern of *The Caretaker* is a double cycle (in this at least it is related to common Absurd dramatic structure) of failure of communication; in each cycle a man turns to another with mistaken trust, not realizing till too late that the person in whom he confides regards him with detachment, contempt, and finally a determination to destroy or at least evict him.

In the first cycle, Aston brings Davies home, offers him a seat, a bit of tobacco, shoes, a place to sleep. At first monosyllabic, Aston becomes increasingly talkative, and makes trivial revelations of things that have apparently stayed in his mind and need to be spoken – for instance, the Guinness they gave him in a thick mug:

I can't drink Guinness from a thick mug. I only like it out of a
thin glass

and the woman who came up to him in the café:

and she said, how would you like me to have a look at your body?. . .
To come out with it just like that, in the middle of this conversation.
Struck me as a bit odd.

These tentative revelations culminate in the long and moving
speech at the end of Act II on his experiences in the asylum, where
he was given shock treatment. From the beginning Davies listens
to him with complete lack of interest or understanding. After
Aston's story of being served the Guinness in the thick mug,
Davies with no sign of having heard him replies:

If only the weather would break! Then I'd be able to get down to
Sidcup!

He shows a little more curiosity in the story about the woman in
the café, but his reply again relates to himself:

They've said the same thing to me. . . There's many a time they've
come up to me and asked me more or less the same question.

As Aston speaks of the shock treatment given to him forcibly, the
spotlight gradually focusses on him; quietly the rest of the room
fades into darkness, so that it and Davies become shadow-like,
a technique which emphasizes Aston's total isolation in his moment
of speaking out. He is indeed "talking to himself", as Davies
suggests later in his version of the incident to Mick:

Couple of weeks ago. . . he sat there, he give me a long chat. . .
about a couple of weeks ago. A long chat he give me. Since then
he ain't hardly said a word. He went on talking there. . . I don't
know what he was. . . he wasn't looking at me. He was talking to
himself! That's all he worries about.

This of course is not wholly true. Aston has been generous to
Davies, has taken sufficient interest in Davies' affairs to ask
questions which Davies persistently evades; but there is a germ
of truth. Aston's confidences have seemed to spring from a deep
need to confide rather than from the topics he and Davies have
been discussing. Ironically, Davies feels his own need for communication; he talks to Mick about his relationship with Aston,
says:

I mean, we don't have any conversation, you see? You can't live in the same room with someone who... who don't have any conversation with you.

With even heavier irony, Davies objects in Act III when Aston slips unseen from the room during the old vagrant's stream of complaints:

Christ! That bastard, he ain't even listening to me!

In the second half of the play, Davies makes a mistake parallel to that of Aston in the first half; he assumes sympathy in Mick, assumes a sense of partnership with him that is of course wildly mistaken. Again ironically he thinks he sees in Mick qualities that do actually exist in Aston:

DAVIES. ... You don't know where you are with him. I mean, with a bloke like you, you know where you are.
MICK *looks at him.*
MICK. Straightforward.
DAVIES. That's it, you're straightforward.

Davies is the only character in the play to ask in so many words for understanding. He does it first in Act II, though not in a cringing way, when he is seeking to come to terms with Mick, and says:

You understand my meaning?

and later:

You know what I'm talking about then?

At the end of the play he again seeks understanding, frantic and abject and wholly too late, from Aston:

But you don't understand my meaning!

and:

Do you see what I'm saying?

Davies, refusing sympathetic hearing to Aston's story, rejected him; the position is exactly reversed at the end of the play, when Aston silently turns his back on Davies' frantic pleading for another chance. It could be said that the characters have returned to the positions they occupied just before the play began, unless one takes the optimistic view that believes Aston really will get on with the task of building the shed, as he says. We can be no more certain of this than we can be certain whether or not Godot

will come; what does seem sure is that Davies is once more homeless and alone.

The distinction between Pinter's use of failure of communication in *The Caretaker* and his other stage plays is that in *The
Caretaker* it is pivotal to the action; in *The Room, The Dumb
Waiter,* and *The Birthday Party* it is not. In these earlier plays,
the isolation of the characters heightens the pity an audience feels
for them, heightens their vulnerability to the situation in which
they find themselves. One feels it is part of the precarious universal
human situation; but isolation does not actually precipitate events,
isolation does not cause the visitation of menace. In *The Caretaker,*
on the other hand, what happens does hinge largely (while
co-existent with greed and insecurity motivation) on two people
seeking, and failing to achieve, communication and sympathetic
understanding. *The Caretaker,* in this pivotal use of failure of
communication, comes closer to the radio plays *A Slight Ache*
and *The Dwarfs,* written, as already suggested, in roughly the
same period as *The Caretaker,* and sharing with it a common
pattern of expulsion of one member of a triangle. It could be
said that in *A Slight Ache* and *The Dwarfs* failure of communication precipitates the "action", such as it is, Edward failing to
communicate with the Matchseller, and Len failing to communicate with Pete and Mark. In the radio plays, however, philosophic
preoccupations tend to outweigh the simpler desire for human
communication; there is a difference of emphasis in the plays.
One could hardly describe *A Slight Ache* as being about Edward's
failure to make friends with the Matchseller.

Pinter is extraordinarily perceptive about man's fear and desire
to know and be known, and in his understanding is a compassion
which has not always been credited to him. One of his most sympathetic portraits of isolation is Meg in *The Birthday Party.* Meg
is truly pathetic, and at the same time too comic for Pinter to be
accused of sentimentalizing her. In Meg, isolation is due in part
to her low intelligence, so that her adored Stanley obviously
finds her boring to talk to, and even Petey prefers to read his
paper rather than listen to her, though he is in his way kindly
and protective towards his wife. This barrier is established in the
opening scene, where Meg talks to Petey in a well-meaning attempt
at communication, trying like any good wife to take an interest in
her husband's career:

MEG. . . . What time did you go out this morning, Petey?

PETEY. Same time as usual.

MEG. Was it dark?

PETEY. No, it was light.

MEG (*beginning to darn*). But sometimes you go out in the morning and it's dark.

PETEY. That's in the winter.

MEG. Oh, in winter.

PETEY. Yes, it gets light later in winter.

MEG. Oh.

Equally well meant, but disastrously unsuccessful, is her gift to Stanley of a boy's drum, in an attempt to compensate him for not having a career as a concert pianist.

Defective intelligence thus cuts across some of Meg's sincere attempts to communicate; but fear also plays its part in isolating her, making her at times refuse to communicate with either Petey or Stanley. Where this fear comes from, one cannot know, but it is rooted deep in her being. Meg, it seems, is afraid of facing up to any unpleasant realities and openly discussing them, and she shows herself to be a practised hand at turning her back on anything uncomfortable. Many Pinter characters yearn nostalgically (and often unconvincingly) for the past, but Meg is most consistent in her references to a cosy, comfortable childhood, to her father who was a "very big doctor"; he did not take her to Ireland but provided a Nanny (who "used to sit up with me, and sing songs to me") and a little room with "pink carpet and pink curtains" and "musical boxes all over the room". Even the frock which she wears to the birthday party, described by Goldberg as "out of this world", was given to her by her father. We may have a shrewd suspicion that Meg's memories are actually fantasies, but memory or fantasy, they indicate her yearning for comfort, companionship, and security. In her dealings with the world of the present, Meg defiantly refuses to face up to unpleasant truths, to admit they exist or talk about them; she becomes almost hysterical as she refuses to let Stanley tell her who "they" are coming for in a wheelbarrow, though her later questions to Petey suggest that she suspects it is Stanley himself. Stanley's story of his career as a concert pianist is ambiguous, to say the least:

STANLEY (*to himself*). I had a unique touch. Absolutely unique. They came up to me. They came up to me and said they were

grateful. Champagne we had that night, the lot. (*Pause.*) My
father nearly came down to hear me. Well, I dropped him a
card anyway. But I don't think he could make it. No, I – I
lost the address, that was it. (*Pause.*) Yes. Lower Edmonton.
Then after that, you know what they did? They carved me up.
Carved me up. It was all arranged, it was all worked out. My
next concert. Somewhere else it was. In winter. I went down
there to play. Then, when I got there, the hall was closed,
the place was shuttered up, not even a caretaker. They'd locked
it up. (*Takes off his glasses and wipes them on his pyjama jacket.*)
A fast one. They pulled a fast one. I'd like to know who was
responsible for that. (*Bitterly.*) All right, Jack, I can take a tip.
They want me to crawl down on my bended knees. Well I can
take a tip. . . any day of the week.

Meg, in her version of the story, modifies it so that in her eyes at
any rate it reflects more credit on Stanley, presumably believing
her own story, in full sincerity.

    MEG (*falteringly.*) In. . .in a big hall. His father gave him cham-
    pagne. But then they locked the place up and he couldn't get
    out. The caretaker had gone home. So he had to wait until the
    morning before he could get out. (*With confidence.*) They were
    very grateful. (*Pause.*) And then they all wanted to give him a
    tip. And so he took the tip. And then he got a fast train and he
    came down here.

Meg has one tell-tale phrase which she uses when she is in doubt;
she pushes aside the doubt with a firm "I know". She knows
for instance that Stanley has a lot of friends, and that the house
is on the list as a good boarding-house, though both suppositions
seem to the audience highly improbable; soon her determined
affirmations come to suggest to the audience that Meg is in fact
doubtful. Imprisoned by her fear of admitting that anything
unpleasant exists, Meg's relationship with the world can only be
evasive, incomplete; her fear, and that of Petey, is used at the end
of the play with poignant effect.

    It is clear, towards the end of the play, that Petey knows or
guesses at least in part what has happened; we hear his knowledge
in his broken cry, "Stan, don't let them tell you what to do!"
as Stanley is carried off by Goldberg and McCann. If he admits
openly that he knows what has happened, Petey might have to do
something about it, so he is content to retire behind his newspaper,
to affirm that he was not at the party, to agree that it must have

been a good evening. Meg's memory is not good, but it is difficult
to believe that she has really forgotten that the previous evening
was not simply a happy birthday party – if nothing else, she might
recollect that Stanley tried to strangle her in the course of it. We
remember that she watched McCann place the drum in Stanley's
path, and that she exclaimed "Ooh!" when Stanley, blindfold,
walked into it and broke it; but now, the morning after, she asks
Petey:

> Why is it broken?

and comments sadly:

> It was probably broken in the party. I don't remember it being
> broken, though, in the party.

Come what may, Meg is resolutely determined that it was indeed
a lovely party, and all is well.

> MEG. Wasn't it a lovely party last night?
> PETEY. I wasn't there.
> MEG. Weren't you?
> PETEY. I came in afterwards.
> MEG. Oh.
> *Pause.*
> It was a lovely party. I haven't laughed so much for years. We
> had dancing and singing. And games. You should have been there.
> PETEY. It was good, eh?
> *Pause.*
> MEG. I was the belle of the ball.
> PETEY. Were you?
> MEG. Oh, yes. They all said I was.
> PETEY. I bet you were, too.
> MEG. Oh, it's true. I was.
> *Pause.*
> I know I was.

The "I know I was", familiar now as a shield against doubt,
gives the lines special significance. The opening scene suggested
Meg's and Petey's isolation from each other; the closing scene
more deeply confirms it.[5]

It is in fact the common pattern of the Pinter play to begin and

---

5. A similar technique is used by Australian author Ray Mathew in his play
A Spring Song. In *A Spring Song,* the phrase "It will be jolly here" occurs
several times, and after the first occurrence is invariably followed by something unpleasant, usually some touch of oppression by the heavy father

end in isolation. In *The Room,* Bert speaks for the first time in the closing moments of the play, but it is speech that reveals his total self-absorption: Riley is dead; and Rose, blinded, is even further cut off from the world than she was in the beginning. In *The Dumb Waiter,* Gus and Ben, as partners, have shared some kind of relationship, but in the end Ben becomes Gus's executioner. In *The Birthday Party,* Stanley has lost his powers of communication; he is speechless and probably almost blind, without his glasses, while Meg and Petey, as we have seen, are left on their own particular islands of non-communication. Edward in *A Slight Ache* stands holding the tray of matches while his wife leads off the Matchseller; and Len in *The Dwarfs* complains "I'm left in the lurch". Davies pleads with a silently unyielding Aston in *The Caretaker;* Max in *The Homecoming* whimpers, moans, and sobs, "I'm not an old man", as he tries to make Ruth aware of him. Disson stares silently and perhaps sightlessly, in *Tea Party,* at the friends and relations he believes to be united against him. The television plays *The Basement, The Lover,* and *The Collection* are less adamant about the isolation of their characters, but they leave us with little confidence in the security of their respective futures. On first impression, *A Night Out* also seems to be an exception to the rule of final isolation, as the Mother forgives her Albert and plans a little holiday with him; but one might say that the strangling silver cord isolates Albert as terribly as any other Pinter character, effectively shutting him off from a normal life. Perhaps the only really happy ending occurs in *Night School,* where the objectionable Walter has successfully dislodged Sally from his room and sits back to enjoy it and the fussing of his elderly aunts, with no competition.

The aspect of Pinter's plays which has probably been most seriously discussed is, not surprisingly, their language.[6] It has

of the family, Mr. Dennison. The words therefore have special significance when they occur right at the end, closing the play, and suggest that in spite of the frantic hopes of the characters and their laughter, life will not be so very jolly in the Dennison household.

6. E.g. John Russell Brown, "Dialogue in Pinter and Others", *Critical Quarterly,* VII, No. 3 (Autumn 1965), 225–43; Peter Davison, "Contemporary Drama and Popular Dramatic Forms", *Aspects of Drama and the Theatre* (Sydney: Sydney University Press, 1965); Martin Esslin, *The Theatre of the Absurd* (London: Eyre and Spottiswoode, 1962); J.R. Taylor, *Anger and After* (London: Methuen, 1962).

been inspected from every angle, analysed in terms of its fidelity to life, its musical qualities, its ancestry in the music halls, and, by no means least important, the words that are not spoken, the revelations that are made silently in pause or gesture. A non-literary fidelity to life may well be one of the first impressions one receives from Pinter's earlier plays, with their realism of repetitions, non sequiturs, and people who think at different speeds (or where one of them has his or her mind on something else) trying to hold a conversation.

> ASTON. You've got to have a good pair of shoes.
> DAVIES. Shoes? It's life and death to me. I had to go all the way to Luton in these.
> ASTON. What happened when you got there, then?
> *Pause.*
> DAVIES. I used to know a bootmaker in Acton. He was a good mate to me.
> *Pause.*
> You know what that bastard monk said to me?
> *Pause.*
> How many more Blacks you got around here then?
> ASTON. What?
> DAVIES. You got any more Blacks around here?
> ASTON (*holding out the shoes*). See if these are any good.
> DAVIES. You know what that bastard monk said to me? (*He looks over to the shoes.*) I think those'd be a bit small.

The point that Pinter often seems to be making in such exchanges is that we understand each other surprisingly well in spite of our lack of accuracy in using language, our lack of logically developed thought, our habit of using the same word to mean many different things. (In the printed version of *The Birthday Party*, the word "nice" appears ten times in the first four pages, with a variety of slightly different meanings.) Up-down is a linguistic absurdity for which Pinter seems to have a special affection:

> MEG. Is Stanley up yet?
> PETEY. I don't know. Is he?
> MEG. I don't know. I haven't seen him down yet.
> PETEY. Well, then, he can't be up.
> MEG. Haven't you seen him down?

It appears again in a revue sketch, *The Black and White,* where
two old women are talking in a milk bar:

> FIRST. . . .That's another all-night bus gone down. (*Pause.*)
> Going up the other way. Fulham way. (*Pause.*) That was a
> two-nine-seven. (*Pause.*) I've never been up that way. (*Pause.*)
> I've been down to Liverpool Street.
> SECOND. That's up the other way.
> FIRST. I don't fancy going down there, down Fulham way, and all
> up there.

Genuine mistakes, through misunderstanding of words, are rare
and comic, as when in *The Birthday Party* Meg becomes coy
because Stanley has said that the fried bread is succulent, protests:

> You shouldn't say that to a married woman.

Later, very revealingly, she mentions the word again, now in her
own mind transferred to herself, and tells him:

> Go on. Calling me that.

Is Pinter's attitude then, like that of the dramatists of the
Absurd, critical of language? If it is, the criticism is sharpest in
the passages which show words to be, as Pinter says, "platitu-
dinous, trite, meaningless",[7] or as Ionesco says "words. . . turned
into shells devoid of meaning".[8] Pinter has not written a sustained
attack on the cliché, such as Ionesco's *The Bald Prima Donna,*
inspired by the strange phrases of the English-French Conversation Manual for Beginners; but he does use the cliché on occasion,
perhaps to point up the emptiness of language, sometimes to
suggest the emptiness, the shallowness of the speaker. Lulu in
The Birthday Party, the morning after the party, upbraids Goldberg in a torrent of clichés:

> You used me for a night. A passing fancy.
> ....
> You made use of me by cunning when my defences were down.
> ....
> You quenched your ugly thirst. You took advantage of me when
> I was overwrought. I wouldn't do those things again, not even
> for a Sultan!

---

7. *Sunday Times,* 4 March 1962, p. 25.
8. Eugene Ionesco, *Notes and Counter Notes* (London: John Calder, 1964),
   p. 185.

There is even:

> You didn't appreciate me for myself. You took all those liberties
> only to satisfy your appetite.

Less amusing, and more critical of language perhaps, are the
clichés in the language of Goldberg. His maxims and autobiographies are made up of disjointed clichés that confuse rather than
enlighten, a confusion that comes to a climax in Act III where he
states his creed and his secret of success to McCann – and then
founders because his platitudes end in the irrevocable revelation
of inner hollowness, and lack of belief in anything:

> Because I believe that the world... (*Vacant*.)....
> Because I believe that the world... (*Desperate*.)....
> BECAUSE I BELIEVE THAT THE WORLD... (*Lost*.)....

Recognizably Absurdist is Pinter's use of proper names to cause
confusion. Riley calls Rose "Sal", and she accepts the title. Is
Goldberg's son Emmanuel, Manny, or Timmy? Both Goldberg's
wife and mother call him "Simey", and he reacts with murderous
rage when McCann uses the name instead of the usual Nat.
On a more naturalistic plane, Seeley and Kedge in *A Night Out*
become confused between Lou Fox and Sandy Foxall, and Davies
in *The Caretaker* tries to hide behind the name "Bernard Jenkins".

It would be easy to read criticism of language into Pinter's
frequent and very clever parodies, parodies of jargon of many
kinds, from the jargon of the house-and-garden type of magazine
(in Mick's description to Davies of his plans for the furnishing of
his dream flat) to legal and public service jargon, perhaps Pinter's
favourite and most frequently-attacked targets. McCann is
soothed and satisfied by a quite meaningless conglomeration of
words ("The main issue is a singular issue and quite distinct from
your previous work. Certain elements, however, might well
approximate in points of procedure to some of your other activi-
ties"); Davies on the other hand is reduced to abject fear as
Mick points out to him the conditions of tenancy of the room:

> On the other hand, if you prefer to approach it in the long-term
> way I know an insurance firm in West Ham'll be pleased to handle
> the deal for you. No strings attached, open and above board,
> untarnished record; twenty per cent interest, fifty per cent deposit;
> down payments, back payments, family allowances, bonus schemes,

remission of term for good behaviour, six months lease, yearly examination of the relevant archives, tea laid on, disposal of shares, benefit extension, compensation on cessation, comprehensive indemnity against Riot, Civil Commotion, Labour Disturbances, Storm, Tempest, Thunderbolt, Larceny or Cattle all subject to a daily check and double check.

One could take the line of argument further by bringing in the tumultuous, seemingly nonsensical speeches, the interrogations and the arias, meaningful to the characters on stage; and beyond these, the enormous importance of the unspoken word, analysed by John Russell Brown in the article cited, where he suggests that Pinter's "dramas cannot be received without a continuous intimation of the unconscious lives of his characters" through trivia revealing unconscious reaction and motivation; he discusses too the pauses that mark "silent interplay of conscious and unconscious motivation" and the way "Pinter's dialogue intimately relates words and gestures, and often progresses from words to gestures". Pinter himself has said:

> I have mixed feelings about words myself. Moving among them, sorting them out, watching them appear on the page, from this I derive a considerable pleasure. But at the same time I have another strong feeling about words which amounts to nothing less than nausea. Such a weight of words confronts us, day in, day out, words spoken in a context such as this, words written by me and others, the bulk of it a stale dead terminology; ideas endlessly repeated and permutated, become platitudinous, trite, meaningless. Given this nausea, it's very easy to be overcome by it and step back into paralysis.[9]

One is far more likely to be conscious, in the plays themselves, of Pinter's pleasure in words than of any feeling of nausea; in fact, though no one could accuse Pinter of being a child-like or unsophisticated playwright, his feeling for words in the early plays is very like the savouring appreciation of them found more frequently in young children than in adults. Pleasure in words permeates even the passages where he is presumably scarifying "stale dead terminology", the parodies of jargon. Mick's long description of his dream flat might well seem to many people to paint a plastic nightmare, and yet the words and phrases have a

9. *Sunday Times,* 4 March 1962, p. 25.

colour, a vividness that is strangely close to poetry. This suggests
the paradox of most writing (certainly Pinter's) that attempts to
show up the thinness and lack of meaning in jargon and cliché –
that is, the heightening process, necessary to throw into relief the
defects being attacked, actually injects life into the language, so
that it becomes itself larger-than-life, attention-catching, and
often very amusing.

It is not common in our time for a playwright to enjoy words for
their own sake, to simultaneously see the funny side of words and
use them with a sense of their power of incantation, as Pinter does.
He has a wonderful sense of the comic absurdity of words, the
exotic-grotesque. The names of tools, he lets us see, really are
rather ridiculous, for instance the jig saw and the fret saw of *The
Caretaker*; for anyone who has been baffled by the terminology
of machinery, even the relatively simple machinery of motor cars,
there is special delight in the "male elbow adaptors, tubing nuts,
grub screws, internal fan washers, dog points, half dog points,
white metal bushes" – not to mention the "lovely parallel male
stud couplings" – of the revue sketch, *Trouble in the Works,*
where the workers go on strike and demand to make brandy balls.
In Edward's catalogue of his cellar in *A Slight Ache*, "Fuchs-
mantel Reisling Beeren Auslese" is side by side with "gin and it".
Place names are used in similar fashion; there is no "quinquereme
of Nineveh from distant Ophir" for Pinter as he piles up his place
names. The location of Stanley's mysterious past was apparently
Basingstoke; and the mecca of Davies' ambitions is Sidcup. Mick,
telling Davies about his "funny resemblance to a bloke I once
knew in Shoreditch", piles up place names, from Aldgate to
Dalston Junction, with buses ("a 38, 581, 30 or 38A") thrown
in for good measure. The effect ranges from comedy to bafflement;
an important by-product is the savour of London, though place
names are not of course the only source of this. No one could
ever doubt where a Pinter play is set.

Pinter's sensitivity to words has led him to experiment constantly
with dialogue, and the kind of dialogue he writes has changed
considerably from the early to later plays. *The Caretaker* is the
last of the plays where one could describe the language as exu-
berant; it is also one of Pinter's most carefully designed plays,
particularly in its sounds, its rhythms. It is not surprising that this
play beyond other Pinter dramas has inspired critics to describe

the Pinter dialogue in musical terms. In particular, word-repetition in *The Caretaker* runs in controlled riot, as the following quite typical passage might suggest. The italics within the dialogue are mine.

MICK. He doesn't *like work.*
    Pause.
DAVIES. Go on!
MICK. No, he just doesn't *like work,* that's his trouble.
DAVIES. Is that a fact?
MICK. It's a terrible thing to have to say about your own brother.
DAVIES. Ay.
MICK. He's just *shy of it.* Very *shy of it.*
DAVIES. I *know that sort.*
MICK. You *know* the *type?*
DAVIES. *I've met them.*
MICK. I mean, I want him to get on in the world.
DAVIES. Stands to reason, man.
MICK. If you got an older brother you want to push him on, you
    want to see him make his way. Can't have him idle, he's only
    doing himself harm. That's what I say.
DAVIES. Yes.
MICK. But he won't buckle down to the *job.*
DAVIES. He don't *like work.*
MICK. *Work shy.*
DAVIES. Sounds *like* it to me.
MICK. You've *met the type,* have you?
DAVIES. *I know that sort. I've met them.*
MICK. Causing me great anxiety. You see, I'm a *working* man; I'm
    a tradesman. I've got my own van.
DAVIES. Is that a fact?
MICK. He's supposed to be *doing a little job* for me. . . I keep him
    here to *do a little job.* . . but I don't *know.* . . . I'm coming to the
    conclusion that he's a slow *worker.*
    Pause.
    What would your advice be?
DAVIES. Well. . . He's a *funny bloke,* your brother.
MICK. What?
DAVIES. I was saying, he's. . . he's a bit of a *funny bloke,* your
    brother.
        MICK *stares at him.*
MICK. *Funny?* Why?
DAVIES. Well. . . he's *funny.* . .
MICK. What's *funny* about him?

> *Pause.*
> DAVIES. Not *liking work.*
> MICK. What's *funny* about that?
> DAVIES. Nothing.
> *Pause.*
> MICK. I don't call it *funny.*

Audiences frequently laugh when the more outrageous repetitions force themselves into notice, and presumably there is some Bergsonian reason for such laughter. Most people repeat themselves, these characters rather more than the audiences which laugh in the theatre, but the real importance of the constant repetitions in *The Caretaker* lies I think not in their "fidelity to life" but in the rhythmic effect they create, echoing drum-like in the mind, with a binding power similar to rhyme or repeated sound in verse. It is quite possible that these constant sound-repetitions, of which there are far more in *The Caretaker* than in any other play, can be related to constantly repeated references to particular objects, either seen directly by the audience (the characters drawing our attention to them) or mentioned by the characters. We are not allowed to forget these objects, ordinary though they are. The shoes, which Davies needs to make his journey to Sidcup, recur through the play so frequently that they have attracted symbolic interpretations relating and comparing them to the boots in *Waiting for Godot.* Among the objects, visible on stage, to which our attention is drawn in the dialogue, are the Buddha; the toaster with which Aston is constantly fiddling; the stove; the bucket hanging ominously overhead. Davies, complaining to Mick that Aston will not give him a bread-knife, repeats the word "knife" over and over again; eight pages later comes his show-down with Aston, and he threatens him with a knife. (He also pulls a knife when Mick menaces him in the darkness with the vacuum cleaner.) Papers seem to be enormously important to each of the characters. Davies talks of his papers at Sidcup; they are mentioned by him and by Mick, and he guards jealously his insurance card. Aston talks of the papers his mother had to sign before he was given shock treatment, and Mick speaks of the deeds that prove his ownership of the room. The dreams of all of them take concrete form: for Aston it is the shed he will build; for Davies, Sidcup where his papers are; and for Mick, unless his tongue is in his cheek, a dream flat. Other word-repetitions are "foreigner" and "Black" (used again and again) and, though not this time exactly a concrete object, "stink" or "stinking", applied normally to Davies; it is Davies' use of the word as a description of Aston's unbuilt shed that is apparently the last straw, and provokes Aston into packing Davies' bag and turning him out. These repetitions of objects and words like "foreigner" and "Black", running through the whole play, are an extension of Pinter's technique on a more confined scale of repeating single words from one sentence to the next. The effects of these over-all repetitions are complex; for instance, the emphasis that is given to certain objects such as shoes, papers, the Buddha, the stove, does help to lend the play an enriching symbolism, even though the author emphatically denies that he deliberately put it there; perhaps equally important is the contribution of these repetitions to the rhythm of the play, working on our emotions, binding and shaping *The Caretaker* into a carefully planned whole.

As a playwright, Harold Pinter has some attitudes at least in common with August Strindberg. An important element of his plays is a humour foreign to Strindberg, but the two playwrights do share a common emphasis on psychic conflict as the essence of drama, with one character (or group of characters) always gaining final ascendancy over another. Beyond this, Pinter's practice in dialogue in many ways fulfills quite precisely Strindberg's theory. This must not be overstated, but the resemblance does go beyond the fact that Strindberg's theory describes the practice of a great deal of modern drama, and Pinter is very much a modern dramatist. Writing in the famous Foreword to *Miss Julie,* Strindberg said:

> . . . I have added a little evolutionary history by making the weaker steal and repeat the words of the stronger, and by making the characters borrow ideas or "suggestions" from one another.10
> I have avoided the symmetrical, mathematical construction of French dialogue, and let people's minds work irregularly, as they do in real life where, during a conversation, no topic is drained to the dregs, and one mind finds in another a chance cog to engage in. So too the dialogue wanders, gathering in the opening scenes

10. *Six Plays of Strindberg,* translated by Elizabeth Sprigge (N.Y.: Doubleday Anchor, 1955), p. 65.

material which is later picked up, worked over, repeated, expounded and developed like the theme in a musical composition.[11]

And if a character from a play may be taken for once as an author's mouthpiece, one might quote the Old Man of *The Ghost Sonata* as expressing a sentiment identical with Pinter's:

OLD MAN. . . . Silence cannot hide anything – but words can.[12]

---

11. *Ibid.,* p. 69.
12. *Ibid.,* p. 292.

4 television plays, the homecoming, and landscape

Kenneth Tynan is reported to have reproached Pinter, early in his career, for dealing with only a limited aspect of the lives of his characters, and omitting "their politics, ideas, even their sex life".[1] A later radio interviewer suggested that as a writer with no social or political commitments, he could be led into an emotional vacuum. Pinter admitted that he had no political commitments, but made a distinction between "political" and "social".

> If I write something in which two people are facing each other over a table... I'm talking about two people living socially, and if what takes place between them is a meaningful and accurate examination of them, then it's going to be relevant to you and to society. This relationship will be an image of other relationships, of social living, of living together...[2]

Pinter is still writing the kind of play in which it would seem to be irrelevant for us to know the political commitments of the characters (if they have any) or their "ideas", even though in

---

1. A radio interview, recorded by Martin Esslin in *The Theatre of the Absurd* (London: Eyre and Spottiswoode, 1962), p. 221.
2. "Pinter on the Screen", Picture Parade 53, B.B.C. Transcription Service.

The Homecoming Teddy is a Ph.D. and a teacher of philosophy, and Lenny, his brother the pimp, ponders the "certain logical incoherence in the central affirmations of Christian theism", and broods, over a liqueur in the Ritz bar, on such philosophical problems as "Take a table. . ." No one, however, would be likely to reproach Pinter any longer for failing to deal with the sex lives of his characters. A witty review of *The Homecoming* described the play in terms of the "mating customs of fighting seals on the beaches of Sakhalin",[3] and in fact most of the plays since *The Caretaker* (the television plays *The Collection, The Lover, Tea Party,* and *The Basement,* and the stage play *The Homecoming*) are in fact bloody sexual battles which leave the vanquished not dead but maimed, bleeding quietly within. The latest play, the difficult, static one-act drama, *Landscape,* first presented not on stage but on B.B.C. radio (25 April 1968) with Peggy Ashcroft and Eric Porter, is a little different: the two speakers do not have sufficient communication to "battle"; the woman neither looks at the man nor seems to hear his voice, while he sees but does not appear to hear her. One might say that this husband and wife, Duff and Beth, are more serious casualties in the sexual conflict, having gone beyond warfare into almost total non-communication and lack of understanding. Pinter has not abandoned his evocation of man's insecurity; he has just extended the area in which it is found. Love as presented by Harold Pinter is no romantic haven of happy ever after, but a treacherously shifting sandbar.

Perhaps after *The Caretaker* Pinter was a little tired of being compared with Beckett, and having his ineffectual heroes set beside Beckett's tramps; perhaps he was tired of writing about the poor and the inarticulate and the down-and-outs. His television play, *The Collection,* shot into a social context as unlike that of the earlier plays as one could imagine – the world of the glossy sophistication of the rag trade. The characters of *The Collection* are beset with secret uncertainties, but for the first time they seem to be in their outward appearance at any rate sophisticated, competent, and successful. There are four characters in a kind of amorous quadrangle: James and Stella, husband and wife, both dress designers; and Harry Kane and his "friend" Bill, also in the fashion business. Harry and Bill share an expensive, elegant

---

3. Ronald Bryden, "A Stink of Pinter", *New Statesman,* LXIX (June 1965), 928.

house in Belgravia, furnished period style; James and Stella have a tasteful contemporary flat in Chelsea. They meet – or rather, James, Bill, and Harry meet, and later Harry and Stella – when James visits Bill and tells him that Stella has confessed she and Bill went to bed together in Leeds, when they were away with dress collections and happened to stay in the same hotel. At first Bill denies even being in Leeds, but when James persists with such details as the yellow pyjamas Bill was allegedly wearing at the time, Bill modifies his story slightly, and suggests that he and Stella just exchanged a few kisses by the lift. James describes how he telephoned to his wife:

> JAMES. Her voice was low. I asked her to speak up. She didn't have much to say. You were sitting on the bed, next to her.
> *Silence.*
> BILL. Not sitting. Lying.

The scene cuts off in blackout. The single word "lying" is emphatic and ambiguous: is Bill lying or telling the truth? James and Harry, the injured parties, both try to discover what happened at Leeds – everything or nothing? Mild flirtation? Or is it all a fantasy of Stella's? Or even a hallucination of James's? The audience is not encouraged to put its trust in the word of any of the characters; one after another they are caught out in untruths, and Bill, the most persistent liar, in several. James's last words to his wife are "That's the truth, isn't it?" and she "looks at him, neither confirming nor denying. Her face is friendly, sympathetic." The scene fades on the four figures sitting in their respective living rooms in the half-light, and the audience knows that Harry and James are doomed to the perpetual frustration of never really knowing the truth.

The situation does not have the sombre Pirandellian suggestion that we can never know the truth about anything, but rather, that in this particular situation the truth will not be known by two of the four characters. The other two know it very well indeed. *The Collection* is a sophisticated and amusing comedy of manners, erected over the familiar Pinter abyss of menace and violence. The adult-childish game, the horse-play, that leads into real violence, is again enacted as James tries to persuade Bill into a mock duel with fruit knives; there is a hint of the familiar Pinter interrogation as Bill trips over the pouffe, and James stands over him

demanding the truth. There is even a suggestion at the beginning
of the play of the old menace figure from outside, as a stranger
phones and asks for Bill, refuses to give his name, and says simply
and chillingly:

Tell him I'll be in touch.

But the stranger turns out to be James – a technique very like
the slightly contrived opening suspense of *The Caretaker*. Of all
the games played by critics, the one writers seem to find most
irritating is a diligent search for resemblances between a new work
and that of some other writer in the past; but it is a game that is
almost irresistible, particularly when the resemblance happens
to be fairly tenuous. Into this category of the tenuous resemblance comes the suggestion that there is perhaps in *The Collection*
a hint of – most surprisingly – Noel Coward. Not the Coward we
now think of as most typical, the scintillating Coward of *Private
Lives,* but Coward obsessed with the decadence and despair
that may lie beneath apparently glamorous and protected lives,
as in *The Vortex*. Normally, it would be ludicrous to compare
Pinter's dialogue, specially the early dialogue with its repetitions,
unfinished sentences, and disparities of intellectual level between
the speakers, with the wit of Coward; but though there is little
Coward wit in *The Collection,* there is a Coward-like sense of
dialogue as duel – cut, thrust, parry, and outwit.

With any Pinter play, one quickly recognizes that, as with the
iceberg, most of what is important is submerged beneath the
surface; one must look for it in what is not said, in gestures
half-restrained. It was probably child's play, and highly amusing,
for Pinter to shape the dialogue of this drama to a kind of modern-
Restoration innuendo, mostly sexual. (No other Pinter play contains so much innuendo, the closest contender being probably *The
Dwarfs*.) Once one begins looking for sexual innuendo in *The
Collection,* such quantities of it may emerge that one may begin
to wonder if one's own imagination has begun to outstrip Pinter's,
or if he has in fact written a considerably bawdy play. There is
the by-play with knives between James and Bill (highly suggestive!), Harry's veiled questioning of Bill as to whether there has
been any dancing or "any gymnastics" in the house; presumably
the lengthy passages about bells and rabbits; and even the food
which Pinter makes – or seems to make – sexually symbolic.

The pouffe, which Bill trips over, is an entirely suitable piece of furniture for Harry's house; and one is tempted to remember that Vivaldi, whose music is played by Bill, composed largely for young women. But probably this is going a little too far, and the Vivaldi is intended only as a contrast to the Charlie Parker sounding so suitably in the other with-it flat. What of the names of the characters? Harry Kane suggests the biblical Cain, who asked: "Am I my brother's keeper?" James's surname is Horne, with ambiguous sexual implications including the traditional horns of the cuckold. Bill Lloyd relates to "lied", very suitably, and to Bill's memorable line of the play: "Not sitting. Lying." Stella is less obvious; perhaps the general association of the name is with the steadfastness of the polar star, and chastity, through possible associations with the Virgin, Stella Maris. Perhaps the name suggests the apparently unwilling sterility of Stella's life, and her kitten (in production guaranteed to steal every scene in which it appears), not only an attractive stage-prop but a substitute child. The play is set in Autumn, the time of decay; the title, *The Collection,* can have a number of reverberations, relating both to the group of people and to the collection of clothes that started it all. It is also quite possible that Pinter himself did not intend any of these word-associations.

With Stella a new character-type emerges, one which becomes very familiar in the later plays: the Pinter Young Woman. In earlier plays, the few young women to appear at all, women such as Lulu in *The Birthday Party* or the girls in *A Night Out,* had relatively minor roles; now they take, if not always the centre of the stage, at least a very prominent position on it. In *A Night Out,* Pinter drew a zestful parallel between mother and whore, as the relentless nagging of the prostitute finally identified her, in Albert's mind, with his mother. (The turning point when Albert is finally driven to desperate self-assertion comes when the prostitute tells him: "I'm a respectable mother, you know, with a child at boarding school.") It is in these terms, mother and whore, that Pinter seems to see his women. In the early plays, where the women were mostly older, colourful, and both comic and pathetic, the mother aspect usually predominated, as in the maternal sluttishness of Meg in *The Birthday Party*; with the younger women of the later plays, the mistress predominates, though the mother does not disappear completely. Sarah in *The Lover* is said to have children

away at boarding school; and it seems at least credible that Ruth
in *The Homecoming* is the mother of children back home in the
States. *The Homecoming* is the play most obviously interested
in this duality of the female role, but the idea is not far from
the heart of the companion television dramas.

Most women would protest that this is an over-simplified and
old-fashioned vision of woman, but Pinter had one vehement
supporter (a woman) in the *Sunday Times*:

> To a woman the play is a detached and witty parable. It meticu-
> lously peels off the layers of hypocrisy concealing the prevailing
> attitudes to woman's morality. It says that in the context of this
> increasingly criminal society a woman can be a wife, mother and,
> if she wishes, a whore. And that men will like her that way. This
> may be a nightmare to some men but many women must have
> felt a sense of relief to discover a modern classic relevant and true
> to life as a woman knows it to be.[4]

Does Pinter say anything more about women than that they are
mothers, wives, and whores? Not, I think, a great deal. His young
women characters have a lot in common. They seem to be sophisticated, attractive, highly sexed. (Or is this last really true?) They
can on occasion break down and show fear or sorrow, as Stella
in *The Collection,* quarrelling with her husband James, cries and
says "I just. . . hoped you'd understand", and Sarah pleads "with
quiet anguish" that her husband will not ask questions and explode
the fantasies on which both their lives are built. But for the most
part Pinter's women are supremely controlled, supremely enigmatic. One may perhaps guess at the motivation of the Pinter male,
or the Pinter older woman; the younger women stand inscrutable,
challenging, and slightly inhuman. However, though Pinter as a
playwright could not be remembered for the creation of his
young women characters, as he might be remembered for the
creation of Davies, they are not simply attractive puppets. They
are saved by their mystery and by a charging vitality that comes to
life in production better than on the printed page. Several of these
young women have been played, dynamically and enigmatically,
by Pinter's talented actress wife, Vivien Merchant – who also
played his early older women, Meg and Rose, as well as the prostitute in *A Night Out.*

---

4. May Bleazard, *Sunday Times,* 4 June 1967.

As has been often pointed out, a startling number of modern playwrights have been drawn to the theme of man's dependence on illusion and dream, his need to retreat to the world of fantasy. Among playwrights who have written on this theme are Ibsen, Pirandello, Synge, O'Neill, Shaw, Miller, Rice, and Albee, to name a few. In the last decade there has risen a sub-species, as it were: plays about dreamers who not only dream dreams but act out their fantasies before us, with like-minded partners, as children play at being grown up, or Batman, or space pilots. Jean Genet is the father of this sub-species, with his plays that straddle the tenuous frontiers between dream and reality. At best painfully moving, Genet's plays are never funny. Also unfunny is the recent Cuban play, Jose Triana's *The Criminals,* in which a brother and two sisters act out what one presumes to be fantasies of killing their parents. However, British playwrights coming after Genet – John Osborne (*Under Plain Cover*), Harold Pinter (*The Lover*), Roger Hirson (*World War 2½*), and Malcolm Quantrill (*Honeymoon*) – have perhaps felt a British need to smile at such unrestrained behaviour, in a slightly self-conscious way. *The Lover* in particular has moments of savage cruelty, but it is also a very witty, crisp, and amusing play.

The beginning of *The Lover* could very well lure an unsuspecting audience into expecting a second drawing-room comedy of menace, perhaps a slightly daring one, as Richard enquires amiably of his wife "Is your lover coming today?" and she replies casually "Mmnn". The first two-fifths of the play continues this impression, as it exposes the rather ordinary (if liberal-minded on the subject of lovers) domestic lives of Richard and Sarah – Richard the sober-suited businessman who arrives home punctually on the stroke of six, Sarah the conscientious housewife who enquires solicitously what the traffic was like on the way home, and reminds her husband about the shears. Richard goes off to work. The door bell rings – obviously, we say, the lover – and in production a kind of alarmed tension rises as Sarah opens the door. But the bell has been a Pinter false alarm; outside is John the milkman who tries to persuade Sarah to take some clotted cream as well as milk, and somehow contrives to make the simple exchange sound suggestive. (In the first edition of the play, his lines, cut for later editions, *were* suggestive.) The door bell sounds again, and this time we are right – Sarah's lover has arrived. It turns out to be her husband Richard, now in suede jacket and no tie, and called by Sarah "Max".

They begin to act out a series of sexual fantasies: first Max is the pest who accosts Sarah, and then the courteous park-keeper who comes to her rescue; Sarah swiftly becomes the seductress trying her wiles in vain on the virtuous park-keeper, who protests that he is married; then in a flash he is the seducer, and she is the victim, protesting:

> I'm a married woman. You can't treat me like this.

They slide from one scenario to the next with the practised ease of a long-established dancing partnership. It is made clear that the two parts of their lives are kept separate and distinct, the life of reality, and the life of fantasy. The barrier is marked by a change of costume: Sarah the mistress in tight frock and high-heeled shoes being distinguished from Sarah the wife in crisp demure frock and low-heeled shoes. They use fantasy, as do Genet's characters, to inject colour and drama into apparently unbearably dull lives, and their fantasies show a Genet-like identification of power and sex on a domestic scale; but unlike Genet's characters, who discuss their motives analytically and rhetorically, Sarah and Richard as "real" beings scrupulously ignore the existence of their fantasy life. Then the barriers between real and fantasy break down. Sarah makes the first slip, by forgetting to take off the high-heeled shoes of her mistress costume. Richard, perhaps tiring of the situation, begins to criticize his mistress to his wife, as simply a "part-time whore" and "too bony"; and, trapped by the rules of the game, Sarah cannot adequately defend herself. Finally Richard as husband demands that she no longer invite her lover to the house; she must give up what he calls "Your debauchery. . . Your life of depravity. Your path of illegitimate lust", and "if I find him on these premises I'll kick his teeth out." For the first time, and in spite of Sarah's initial anguished protest, they launch straight into their fantasy from real life, without the pretence of Richard coming to the house as another person. The best that Sarah can do to smooth over the fact that they have not changed costume is to comment on the strangeness of their clothing – "Why are you wearing this strange suit, and this tie?" – and offer to change her own clothing. The play ends with what might be called a reconciliation, as they kneel together on the floor and Richard murmurs:

You lovely whore.

But it is not a reassuring ending; something has gone wrong, though it is not quite clear what this is. From one point of view, Sarah has just managed to save from destruction "the game" which means so much to her, just managed to divert Richard from smashing their fantasy to pieces. What however of tomorrow or the day after? What will happen to their relationship if the fantasy does break down? Another point of view could suggest that Richard has made a praiseworthy attempt to break through the make-believe to reality, perhaps to put their relationship on a firmer footing, and has been defeated.

Pinter's plays have something in common with Genet's in their underlying savagery; even more in their evocation of the loneliness of the characters, particularly as the curtain falls. Genet's *Death Watch* ends with the words of Lefranc:

I really am alone.

Solange's speech at the end of *The Maids* may seem to have a joyous ring as she stands alone on stage and cries:

We are beautiful, joyous, drunk and free!

But it is an ironic joy, for she stands with the body of her dead sister behind her, and the inevitable prospect of prison looming ahead. *The Balcony* closes with Irma alone on stage, extinguishing the lights, "alone, mistress and assistant mistress of this house and of myself", while her lover prepares for an eternity within a mausoleum. *The Blacks* and *The Screens* provide a variation in that the characters walk away from the audience; in *The Blacks* they specifically turn their backs on the audience, and the effect in production can be that the audience feels itself alone, deliberately rejected. Mechanically it might seem that Pinter's *The Lover* is, as a play in which people consciously act out fantasies, the closest of his plays to Genet's; but perhaps in fact the early comedies have more in common with Genet. With Genet's dramas one is never quite sure where lies the exact borderline between "reality" and "fantasy", or if indeed there is ever any "reality" at all. In *The Balcony* it would seem that while Madame Irma's clients act out their erotic fantasies in the brothel, real gunfire sounds intermittently from without; but soon one begins to suspect that the entire action, reality and fantasy both, is part of a single dream. Pinter's "reality" is much more real than that of Genet, if Genet ever does present reality at all; but in the early plays, the mingling of real with nightmare-fantastic, the unexplained, does result in something a little like Genet's dreams, though with of course a humour and ear for "the way people speak" alien to Genet's more sombre rhetoric.

With the change in the social, educational, and financial level of his characters, the language of Pinter's plays inevitably changed too. The non sequiturs faded, the passages between people thinking at different speeds. Even the repetitions, which had risen to a crescendo in *The Caretaker,* became infrequent, reduced to the occasional repetitions of repeated speech, or sometimes repetitions to emphasize a point; no longer are there repetitions predominantly for the sake of sound. The only repetition one might remember from *The Lover* would probably be the following, memorable not so much for the actual repetition as for the excruciating pun:

> RICHARD. The trouble with this room is that it catches the sun so
>   directly, when it's shining. You didn't move to another room?
> SARAH. No. We stayed here.
> RICHARD. Must have been blinding.
> SARAH. It was. That's why we put the blinds down.
> RICHARD. The thing is it gets so awfully hot in here with the blinds
>   down.

With *Tea Party* and *The Basement* comes a change in Pinter's use of dialogue. *The Collection* and *The Lover,* proceeding in brief, rapidly changing scenes, using visual effect and the emphasis of close-up, are essentially television plays, but they can without too much effort be adapted to the stage; and words are still important. The same cannot be said of *Tea Party* and *The Basement,* where almost everything that is important happens in pictures rather than words. What one remembers of these plays in television production is how things looked, rather than words spoken. This means that the author is using his medium, the television screen, to its maximum efficiency, and it is probably meaningless to add that the sparseness of dialogue makes these plays less than usually satisfying on the printed page. One must also add that, in spite of obvious difficulties of adaption, both *Tea Party* and *The Basement* were staged in 1968 in New York—with, apparently, some success. The critic of the *New York Times* reports:

If Pinter had wanted to write these plays primarily for the stage, they would, I am sure, have been very different from their present form. Yet, and Pinter is always full of surprises, it is absolutely amazing how well both stand up in a theater. With virtually no changes to the script, but a staging that carefully parallels so far as possible television effects, the plays make a finely mysterious evening in the theater.[5]

However, even in production *Tea Party* and *The Basement* are probably Pinter's least satisfying and most inflated dramas, even though *Tea Party* does happen to be headed by the numerically impressive statement that it was "commissioned by the sixteen member countries of the European Broadcasting Union, to be transmitted by all of them under the title, *The Largest Theatre in the World*". The enthusiastic *New York Times* reviewer admits that they are "minor Pinter", but adds:

> Pinter is one of the most important English-speaking playwrights since O'Neill, and minor Pinter is better than major almost anyone else.[6]

Tea Party unfolds with the relentless if crazy inevitability of a nightmare. Disson is the head of a firm of sanitary engineers:

> We manufacture more bidets than anyone else in England. . . It's almost by way of a mission.

Simultaneously he acquires a new secretary, Wendy, who left her previous position because her employer "never stopped touching me", and a new wife, Diana – together with Diana's brother, Willy. Disson takes Willy into the firm, and Diana comes too, as her brother's secretary. The play traces Disson's loss of ascendancy, in his office and in his home, his growing sense that everyone round him is in conspiracy against him, till he finally collapses (speechless as the tormented Stanley in *The Birthday Party*) at the family tea party in his office with which the play closes. The particular gimmick of the play is the way the camera silently suggests some of the stresses bearing down on Disson. Beginning impartially, the camera gradually begins to alternate between the objective view and that of Disson himself. From Disson's point of view we see the two table tennis balls that fly past his ears in the game with

---

5. *New York Times,* 16 October 1968, p. 40.
6. *Ibid.*

Willy while everyone assures him there was only one; we see close-ups of the vital areas of Wendy's considerable charms; and the screen blacks out as vision apparently blacks out for Disson. At the final grim tea party, Disson sits with a bandage covering the eyes he now mistrusts. Part of the time we see the whole room, the objective point of view; interspersed is Disson's "point of view" in which, though his eyes are covered, he apparently sees what is happening, sees his associates in conspiratorial groups, sees Willy fondling Wendy and Diana as they lie on the desk– but hears nothing. Disson collapses; they finally manage to raise him and cut the bandage from his eyes, his eyes are open, but he does not speak. Has Disson gone mad, or very close to it? Or is it just possible that he is the victim of some weird conspiracy? Why does Willy hand him at the tea party a table tennis ball? The play does have some of the unnerving terror of a nightmare, and it traces the steps of Disson's disintegration as businessman, husband, and father, with admirable economy. And yet the final impression is that it is a slight play, making a point that has been made with greater depth before – by Pinter and others.

In terms of written words on the page, *The Basement* is a very short play, about half the length of *Tea Party*; yet in its first 1967 production by the B.B.C. it gave the impression, after an arresting opening, of going on a little too long. If pictures asserted at least equal rights with words in *Tea Party,* in *The Basement* they almost replace them. The play is a return to the theme (which perhaps Pinter never really left?) of dominance within a room; as in the short story, *The Examination,* it shows two men in a cycle of domination in the room, first one in possession and then the other, but this time with the added complication of possession of the woman also.

The play opens, on a rainy winter night, as a man, Stott, stands outside the door of a basement flat; behind him huddles a girl, Jane. The next shot shows us the interior of the flat, a large and comfortably if prosaically furnished bed-sitting room, where Law sits reading a Persian love manual "with illustrations". The doorbell rings, Law answers it, greets Stott as a friend whom he hasn't seen for years, and invites him in – Jane for the moment is out of sight. Law invites Stott to stay, says he has a camp bed he can fit up, and Stott asks if his friend can come in also. Once Jane is in the room, Stott turns down the lamps, Jane rapidly removes her clothes, and climbs naked into the large double bed, followed by Stott, now also naked. For a time Law tries to keep the conversation going, finally giving up the attempt as the couple make love, ignoring him; and he goes back to reading *The Persian Manual of Love*. Jane and Stott stay on, tension between the three building through the changing seasons of winter and summer. Stott, the dominant one, alters the decor of the room to modern Swedish; Jane whispers seductively to Law:

> Why don't you tell him to go? We had such a lovely home. . . Tell him to go. . . Then we could be happy again. Like we used to.

Law tells Stott:

> She betrays you. She has no loyalty.

For a moment it seems as if Stott is dying, but he recovers, and the decor of the room changes once again startlingly to baroque, ornate with tapestries, oval Florentine mirrors, marble pillars and carved golden chairs. In one of the most tense (and almost wordless) scenes of the play, Stott and Law play cricket, Stott bowling with large marbles while Law bats with his recorder. Then the room becomes bare, the men face each other with broken milk bottles, while Jane prepares coffee – for two. The broken milk bottles thrust together, smashing, music sounds from the turntable, *Girl With the Flaxen Hair*; and then the scene is as it was in the beginning, a man and a girl outside in the rain, and a second man inside, reading by the fire. This time however it is Law who is outside, Law who knocks, and Stott who answers the door to greet with pleasure his long-lost friend.

Even more than *Tea Party, The Basement* suggests a dream, pictorial rather than verbal, like most people's real-life dreams. It was, apparently, originally conceived as a film script but was first produced by the B.B.C. In this production the elaborate, changing set took over the leading role, as it would almost inevitably do. The best scene was the cricket match, like all Pinter's "games" concealing a deeper struggle and ending in violence, with the marbles which Stott uses instead of a cricket ball as he bowls to Law crashing into the wall, the window, Law's knee, the fish tank – breaking it so that "dozens of fish swim across the marble tiles" – till finally a marble strikes Law's forehead, and he drops. *The Basement* is by no means the only Pinter play to move from reality into what seems like fantasy, but it makes the transition more rapidly than most. It has been suggested more than once, though the idea has not yet been explored at length, that Pinter's techniques may have been influenced by his experiences as an actor in improvisation sessions. If this is true of any of the plays, it is most likely to be true of *The Basement*. Harold Pinter played Stott in the first production of the play, and gave interesting proof to audiences that he is a highly competent actor as well as playwright and producer.

Only occasionally does television inspire profundity, and Pinter's television plays are taut, often witty, always highly sensitive to the medium, and on the whole more superficial than his earlier stage and radio plays. (A substantial number of Pinter critics would of course deny that one should look at all for "meanings" in Pinter's work.) The plays are linked in their variety by a concern with love or lust, love not binding but disruptive and uncertain, love changing and shaping new alliances. His latest full-length stage play, *The Homecoming,* bears a very similar message.

The title, *The Homecoming,* is like most of Pinter's titles ironically innocuous, with echoes of the return of the prodigal. Ostensibly the homecoming is that of Teddy, now a Ph.D. and a philosophy teacher in an American university, to the bosom of his North London family, after an absence of six years. Teddy is accompanied by his attractive wife, Ruth, apparently an ex-model ("a photographic model for the body") and mother of their three sons at home in America. The family Teddy has come home to visit consists of his father, the aging tearaway Max; his weakly pathetic uncle Sam, "the best chauffeur in the firm"; and his two brothers, Lenny, a pimp by profession, and Joey, the baby of the family, slow-thinking, a demolition worker and would-be professional fighter. In the end the homecoming proves to be a homecoming for Ruth rather than Teddy. She has never met her husband's family before, but she and they recognize instant kinship; as Max says:

You're kin. You're kith. You belong here.

He is right; she belongs to their jungle world of action, rather than to Teddy's academic non-involvement; and in the end she stays while Teddy takes his suitcases to catch the plane back to America. It is intended by the family that Ruth will earn her keep, of course, and – apart from her providing relaxation for the family – Lenny will settle her in one of his quiet retreats for businessmen in Greek Street, after, as Ruth insists, "all aspects of agreement and conditions of employment" have been "clarified to our mutual satisfaction". The play ends with a kind of tableau: Sam lies apparently unconscious on the floor; Ruth sits relaxed in her chair, stroking Joey's hair as he kneels at her feet; Lenny watches quietly; and Max, suddenly suspicious that he will be left out of things, crawls sobbing round Ruth's chair:

> I'm not an old man... Do you hear me?... Kiss me.

Pinter himself has emphasized that Ruth is victor.

> If this had been a happy marriage it wouldn't have happened. But she didn't want to go back to America with her husband, so what the hell's she going to do? She's misinterpreted deliberately and used by this family. But eventually she comes back at them with a whip. She says "if you want to play this game I can play it as well as you." She does not become a harlot. At the end of the play she's in possession of a certain kind of freedom. She can do what she wants, and it is not at all certain she will go off to Greek Street. But even if she did, she would not be a harlot in her own mind.[7]

Most of Pinter's dramas involve families and family life, and he can hardly be accused of sentimentalizing it, as he probes the tensions of daily trivia. In this he is not alone among contemporary playwrights. R.F. Storch points out that "the London stage since 1945 (to look no further) has been very much occupied with the family as a trap-door to the underworld".[8] Pinter's plays, he suggests, "are largely about the running away from certain family situations".[9] His married couples either rub along, like Meg and Petey of *The Birthday Party,* or indulge in desperate, merciless infighting, the custom of most of his younger couples. There is no sense of full, sympathetic communication between husband and wife. The most favourable family relationship seems to be between siblings. There is surely quiet affection and silent understanding between Mick and Aston in *The Caretaker,* and Disson's twin sons

---

7. "Probing Pinter's Play" (interview with Henry Hewes), *Saturday Review,* L (8 April 1967), 57.

8. "Harold Pinter's Happy Families", *Massachusetts Review,* VIII (Autumn 1967), 703.

9. *Ibid.,* p. 704.

in *Tea Party,* John and Tom, seem to be in complete harmony, so that neither of them will make even the most trivial observation without calling on the other for confirmation. Lenny in *The Homecoming* has an elder-brother protectiveness towards Joey, and his gentle prodding of Joey to tell the story of the last bird he had (when Lenny and Joey took two girls away from their escorts and presumably raped them – evidence that Joey is "a bit of a knockout when he gets going") is like a wildly bizarre parody of a child being persuaded to recite for visitors. Mr. Kidd in *The Room* speaks favourably of his sister, and Diana and her brother Willy are perfectly attuned in *Tea Party,* infuriating Disson with the shared memories from which he is excluded. Child-parent relationships in Pinter's plays are more ambiguous. There are no very young children in Pinter's plays to date, but the characters tend to remember their childhood in the rosiest and most sentimental terms, as a time of ultimate security. We may not always believe that their memories are true. For Meg in *The Birthday Party* childhood was a time when "I was cared for, and I had little brothers and sisters in other rooms, all different colours"; for Goldberg in the same play it was a period of "Hot water bottles. Hot milk. Pancakes. Soap suds. What a life." Even Max in *The Homecoming* sentimentally remembers his father – or does his last "I remember my father" suggest concealed hostility?

> He used to come over to me and look down at me. My old man did. He'd bend right over me, then he'd pick me up. I was only that big. Then he'd dandle me. Give me the bottle. Wipe me clean. Give me a smile. Pat me on the bum. Pass me around, pass me from hand to hand. Toss me up in the air. Catch me coming down. I remember my father.

All three of these sentimentalists are quite unreliable. Meg as we have seen has no sure grip on the truth and will go to any lengths to protect herself from unpleasant reality; Goldberg gives very varied versions of his past and name; and Max can change his story of times gone by more blatantly than either of them. One moment he recalls the time when his wife was alive and the children young in the most glowing family-story terms; the next he is raging that he had "a crippled family, three bastard sons, a slutbitch of a wife". His rose-coloured vision of the happy family relationship between them, long ago, is undermined by Lenny's contemptuous parody of a childhood plea at the beginning of the play:

> Oh, Daddy, you're not going to use your stick on me, are you?. . .
> It wasn't my fault, Dad, honest. Don't clout me with that stick,
> Dad.

Somehow this rings truer than Max's vision of the past, with the children "their hair shining, their faces pink", kneeling at their parents' feet.

For Pinter's characters, parental authority and influence remain alive and dominant even when the parents themselves are apparently dead. Adult Pinter characters have a tendency to talk about their parents, to think of them in the most unlikely contexts, particularly their mothers. Gus remembers his mother, during the quarrel with Ben in *The Dumb Waiter* over the correctness of light-the-kettle or light-the-gas, remembers her with the air of one casting around for an ultimate authority to support him:

> GUS. I bet my mother used to say it.
> BEN. Your mother? When did you last see your mother?
> GUS. I don't know, about –
> BEN. Well, what are you talking about your mother for?

Mr. Kidd in *The Room* remembers his mother, though vaguely:

> I think my Mum was a Jewess. Yes, I wouldn't be surprised to
> learn that she was a Jewess. She didn't have many babies.

Pinter parents can hurt or betray, at least from the child's point of view: Rose seems terrified when Riley tells her "your father wants you to come home"; Stanley of *The Birthday Party* is sufficiently hurt that his father did not come to his concert, if indeed there was a concert, to make excuses for him; Aston's mother signed the form giving "them" authority to use shock treatment on her son in *The Caretaker* – or at least Aston says she did. Jessie of *The Homecoming,* who taught her sons "all the morality they know", is the most omnipresent, seemingly influential, and yet ambiguous of the off-stage parents. Her husband Max describes her as "the backbone to this family. . . a woman with a will of iron, a heart of gold, and a mind"; at the same time, "even though it made me sick just to look at her rotten, stinking face, she wasn't such a bad bitch". To Sam, she was "a very nice companion to be with". Her sons also mention her, in a way that reveals consciousness of Jessie and her influence, but with attitudes

that are difficult to assess. Lenny tells Ruth not to call him Leonard
because "that's the name my mother gave me" (a reminiscence
of Goldberg's fury at being called "Simey" by McCann?), and
Teddy explains to Ruth how they knocked down a wall to enlarge
the sitting room – "The structure wasn't affected, you see. My
mother was dead." Lenny silences his father in an argument by
putting to him "a question I've been meaning to ask you for some
time. That night. . . you know. . . the night you got me. . . that
night with Mum, what was it like? Eh? When I was just a glint
in your eye." An anonymous *Time* critic once suggested that
Pinter's plays were concerned only with the "sealed nursery-
dungeon of fears",[10] and he suggested that Pinter must break
out and beyond this to achieve real stature. His judgment may
still be right; but to date, Pinter's moments of sharpest perception
have come as his adult characters act out unresolved childhood
conflicts; and their ambiguous attitudes to parents and childhood
seem to suggest a tussle between memory of life as it was and life
as they would have wished it to be.

Pinter's earlier plays touched on family life; *The Homecoming*
is about family life, or rather, as Pinter would insist, the life of a
particular family.[11] *The Homecoming* has proved a perplexing
and controversial play, partly because most of us, in spite of
warnings from the author, have once again tried to read complex
"meanings" and symbol and allegory into it. Though it might be
difficult to be quite confident what the play says, and even more
difficult to assess just how good a play it is, it is perfectly easy to
enjoy the way conventional family values and conventional family
attitudes are turned, outrageously, on their heads. Lenny can
without a quiver take over Teddy's wife and yet express passionate
moral indignation because Teddy eats the cheese roll Lenny has
left in the sideboard for himself. Max feels outraged when Teddy
rejects his suggestion that he contribute to Ruth's support when
she stays with the family, tells him:

> You lousy stinkpig. Your mother would drop dead if she heard
> you take that attitude

and it is expected by all of them that Teddy will do his share as

---

10. "Pinter Patter", *Time,* LXXX (7 December 1962), 54.
11. "Probing Pinter's Play", *Saturday Review,* L (8 April 1967), 57.

publicity agent for Ruth's talents, back home in the States. There
is a touch of Joe Orton in this explosion of established institution,
and one remembers how in *Entertaining Mr. Sloane* a family also
does battle for a sexually desirable stranger, till a solution is
reached with a businesslike arrangement in clearly defined terms
(as in *The Homecoming*) which Ed puts down to "my experience
at the conference table". The tone of the two plays is, however,
quite different. For all his savagery, Orton often burlesques, plays
openly for laughs; Pinter, more subtle, does not clown. *The
Homecoming* demands (and received, in its splendid Royal Shakespeare Company production) a deadly seriousness of approach
from the characters as they speak their incredible lines, casualness
and sometimes even drawing-room formality of manner belying
the anarchic behaviour and sentiments being enacted. Act II
opens with an almost Victorian family tableau as coffee is handed
round and politely commented on – and the scene leads diretly
into guerilla warfare. Teddy puts to Ruth the family's proposition
that she stay with them and work as a whore, and sounds exactly
like a man suggesting to his wife that she spend a couple of weeks
in the country with an aunt:

> Ruth. . . the family have invited you to stay, for a little while
> longer. As a. . . as a kind of guest. If you like the idea I don't mind.
> We can manage very easily at home. . . until you come back.

In the same terms she replies:

> How very nice of them.

Pinter has rejected symbolic and Freudian interpretations of
The Homecoming, and says simply:

> It's about love and lack of love. The people are harsh and cruel
> to be sure. Still, they aren't acting arbitrarily but for very deep-
> seated reasons.

Asked if the characters represented universal forces in modern
society, Pinter replied:

> I was only concerned with this particular family. I didn't relate
> them to any other possible or concrete family. I certainly didn't
> distort them in any way from any other kind of reality. . . . The
> whole play happens on a quite realistic level from my point of view.

When it was suggested that the family might represent a disintegration into pure evil, he said:

> There's no question that the family does behave very calculatedly
> and pretty horribly to each other and to the returning son. But
> they do it out of the texture of their lives and for other reasons which
> are not evil but slightly desperate.12

The actors who took part in the Royal Shakespeare Company
production insist on the reality of the characters, and Michael
Craig, who played Teddy, declares that Teddy is the most violent
of them all.

> Teddy is probably the most violent of them all, but his violence
> is controlled. They play this awful game with him to try and make
> him break, and he turns it round. He shoots it right at his father.
> He says, "I'll call your bluff. If you want a woman in the house,
> here she is if she wants to stay. He's an awful man, Teddy. He's
> rationalized his aggressions, but underneath he's Eichmann.13

The essential fact about the family, before the advent of Ruth,
is that it is a womanless family, a family without woman either
as wife, mistress, or mother, to love or be loved or simply to do
the washing up. The essential fact about Ruth – in fact almost the
only thing we can guess confidently about her previous existence –
is that her marriage is not satisfying, and that the life in America
which to Teddy is apparently stimulating and successful, to Ruth
suggests sterility: rock and sand and insects. Lacking love, Ruth
and the family confront each other, and decide that each can
satisfy the other's needs. Their actions seem incredible because
they are appallingly honest, simple and direct in working out the
desired solution. The difficulty of the play lies not with Ruth or
the family, but with the enigmatic Teddy. How is an audience
intended to react to his withdrawal and apparent defeat? Without
being sure of this, it is difficult to know what (if anything) the
play intends to say *about* love and lack of love.

Another way of looking at this play is to see it as a conflict
between active and passive, or perhaps more accurately between
the openly aggressive and those who control aggression under
apparent passivity. The characters of *The Homecoming* fall into
two main groups, introduced in Act I, of active and apparently
passive. The passive characters are Teddy and Sam, the lookers-on
at life. Teddy, the more highly educated, is also the more explicit

---

12. *Ibid.*
13. *Ibid.*

about his point of view. He is an academic and a man who looks on and criticizes the works of others rather than creating himself, and he states his position in one of the key speeches of the play. The pressures on Teddy to become involved in what is happening, the loss of his wife, are mounting. Ruth has danced with Lenny, rolled off the sofa with Joey, declared her alliance with the world of action. Her tone of voice has been changing, becoming more aggressive, till finally she addresses her husband, asking him directly:

> Have your family read your critical works?

Teddy's long speech is a revelation of his creed, of what is important to him, and could almost be compared to Aston's moment of speaking out at the end of Act II of *The Caretaker*:

> You wouldn't understand my works. You wouldn't have the faintest idea of what they were about. You wouldn't appreciate the points of reference. You're way behind. All of you. There's no point in my sending you my works. You'd be lost. It's nothing to do with the question of intelligence. It's a way of being able to look at the world. It's a question of how far you can operate on things and not in things. I mean it's a question of your capacity to ally the two, to relate the two, to balance the two. To see, to be able to *see*! I'm the one who can see. That's why I can write my critical works. Might do you good. . . . have a look at them. . . see how certain people can view. . . things. . . how certain people can maintain. . . intellectual equilibrium. Intellectual equilibrium. You're just objects. You just. . . move about. I can observe it. I can see what you do. It's the same as I do. But you're lost in it. You won't get me being. . . I won't be lost in it.

His only retaliation for the loss of his wife is to steal Lenny's cheese roll. Typically, the sign of tension between Teddy and Lenny is wordless, oblique: the cigars of both men go out, in the scene where Ruth begins at last to "speak out", glancing at her past and indicating recognition of kinship in the family circle.

The second passive character in *The Homecoming* is Sam. Sam did not even kill anyone in the war. The chief target for Max's incessant sarcasm at Sam's expense it that Sam has never married. Sam's carefully controlled replies to queries whether or no he has been "banging away at your lady customers" would do credit to a nice but determinedly broad-minded spinster, though just occasionally the strain shows through. Max enlarges on Sam's passivity to suggest that he will "bend over for half a dollar on Blackfriar's Bridge", a charge indignantly repudiated by Sam. Just as Teddy insists that Ruth is the ideal wife and mother, and that she has always been as she is now, so Sam manages to idealize his memory of his late sister-in-law Jessie as "a charming woman", a "very nice companion to be with", whom he once or twice drove in his cab and for whom he bought a cup of coffee. This idealization manages to overlook or submerge the fact that "MacGregor had Jessie in the back of my cab as I drove along", until Sam is subjected to the strain of seeing Ruth, the second Jessie, show herself unmistakably a tart; then he blurts out the truth about Jessie and MacGregor. Sam feels an instinctive kinship with Teddy, and suggests to him:

> Why don't you stay for a couple more weeks, eh? We could have a few laughs.

The aggressive characters are headed by Lenny, whose quiet brutality dominates. Lenny does not normally find it necessary to display his strength in words; the closest he comes to it is in two long speeches to Ruth, the male showing off before the female, as he tells her about the "certain lady" who "came up to me and made me a certain proposal" – as she was both importunate and (he decided) diseased, he contemplated killing her, but to save himself tension and the bother of getting rid of the corpse, he "just gave her another belt in the nose and a couple of turns of the boot and sort of left it at that". The second story concerns the old lady who asked him to move a mangle; it proved heavier than he expected but "as I was feeling jubilant with the snow-clearing I just gave her a short-arm jab to the belly and jumped on a bus outside". Strength in Pinter is normally laconic; those who are most effective talk least. Lenny's dominance over his father is established in the opening scene, his contemptuous brevity contrasting with the old man's ineffectual stream of abuse. Later, in this scene where Lenny tells his tales of prowess to Ruth, she establishes a kind of superiority over him with her brief practical comment on the first narrative ("How did you know she was diseased?") and her complete lack of comment on the second. It is not surprising to learn that Ruth was born "quite near here". Joey, though not very bright, is also on the side of strength, and his furious resentment at having to share Ruth with anyone, even Teddy, is in pointed contrast to Teddy's apparent apathy. Finally there is Max, one of Pinter's most colourful stage monsters, vividly larger than life, talking longer and louder than anyone, still lusting for life but growing old, so that the mere effort to knock down members of his family with his stick almost makes him collapse. As with most Pinter old men, including Davies of *The Caretaker,* Max's claim to strength now lies in past glories and large claims. One quality the active and passive characters share: each character is completely self-centred, out for his own advantage, and without compassion. The closest approach to kindliness in the play comes out in Lenny's apparent affection for Joey, and Sam's fellow-feeling for Teddy.

As almost every critic has commented, Act I of *The Homecoming* is pure exposition, almost static; all the action takes place in Act II, but it would not be comprehensible without the information given in Act I. Act I brings the characters on stage and displays them, predominantly in terms of their strengths and weaknesses – in their peck order, in fact. By the end of Act I, the audience has a fair idea of the strength relationship between the characters, though as yet very little idea how they will use it. In the opening scene Lenny effortlessly and quietly dominates Max, who rages futilely "I could have taken care of you, twice over", and comforts himself with boasting of his "instinctive understanding of animals". The next contender to enter the arena is Sam, lower down the power scale than Max. Lenny treats him with contemptuous politeness; Max makes up for his defeat at Lenny's hands by assaulting Sam with aspersions on his ability as a chauffeur and his dubious sexual prowess. Last on stage is Joey, slow but apparently confident in his physical strength, and unperturbed by Max's suggestion that his trouble as a boxer is that he does not know how to defend himself or how to attack.

After a brief blackout, we meet Teddy and Ruth, and Pinter demonstrates with the most admirable economy the strength-relationship between them. Teddy is a fusser, an ineffectual would-be organizer; Ruth quietly resists his organizing with what seems very like concealed irritation, finally deciding to go for a walk in the fresh air. Teddy is left alone, and there follows a very funny version of a situation familiar in Pinter, one character talking frantically and losing control of a situation while his more taciturn opponent assumes it. Lenny enters the room and sees Teddy, and according to the stage directions, stands watching him, but it is Teddy who speaks first. Though Teddy has been away for six years, Lenny shows complete lack of curiosity or surprise at seeing him; Teddy has to ask all the questions that might in the circumstances have been expected to come from his brother, and in the end even has to volunteer, unasked, the information that he himself is keeping well. Perhaps reassured that Teddy has not come home seeking assistance of any kind, Lenny goes so far as to offer a hand with the suitcases or a glass of water. Teddy goes off to bed, Ruth enters, and this time it is Lenny who speaks first. For the first time in the play he becomes almost talkative, and their skirmish over a glass of water might be said to end in a draw. Ruth's meeting with the rest of the family takes place the following morning; not surprisingly her encounter with Max begins with wind and fury on his side, his insistence that she is a "stinking pox-ridden slut", to be resented because "I've never had a whore under this roof before. Ever since your mother died." Soon this collapses into his acceptance of her as a mother, and the act concludes with his apparently delighted discovery that Teddy "still loves his father!" The clan has gathered.

In Act II things happen, every step the logical result of seeds sown in Act I. It soon becomes clear that Ruth will change loyalties. Normally given to watching and speaking in brief sentences, she makes one comparatively long speech, her moment of speaking out as Teddy is to speak later; it is a speech that asserts her belief in the superiority of action over words:

> Look at me. I... move my leg. That's all it is. But I wear... underwear... which moves with me... it... captures your attention. Perhaps you misinterpret. The action is simple. It's a leg... moving. My lips move. Why don't you restrict... your observations to that? Perhaps the fact that they move is more significant... than the words which come through them. You must bear that... possibility... in mind.

The crisis of the play occurs just before the halfway mark of Act II, where Ruth asks Teddy if his family has read his critical works and he proclaims his refusal to be involved. Though this is the turning point, tension does not perceptibly drop because the situation becomes increasingly outrageous, and the climax of it, Ruth's acceptance of her new career, is not reached till the final

moments. Only then is the battle over. But where is the victory?
On the surface, Teddy, losing his wife with contemptibly little
effort to retain her, has been defeated by the family; perhaps Sam,
stretched unconscious on the floor, might seem to be a visible
symbol of the defeat of the weak. On the other hand, Teddy is
also a victor, in that he has, against the greatest odds, avoided
involvement – just as he intended. The only hint that he may
feel pain at the loss of his wife is the fact that it is only to her he
fails to say a polite good-bye as he leaves.

At the time of writing, *The Homecoming* is Harold Pinter's latest
full-length play. The one-act play, *Landscape,* has been presented
on radio but not on any major stage,[14] though it was written for
the stage. *Landscape* shows Pinter turning aside from the extreme
clarity and precision of *The Homecoming,* and it is probably his
least "commercial" play outside *The Dwarfs.* In the helpful light
of future plays, the beginnings of a new kind of Pinter writing may
be later seen to be buried in it, but at the moment it seems to be
a turning backward, a return to the failure of communication
theme and to a style of drama reminiscent of Beckett (*Happy Days*
and *Play*) which seems to have generally spent itself in the theatre.
In *Landscape* absolutely nothing happens save that a man and a
woman speak aloud their thoughts, their quite separate preoccupations, the woman neither hearing nor seeing the man, the man
speaking to the woman sometimes but not hearing her. The woman
is the more sensitive, the more perceptive and sensuous, and concerned principally with memories of love; the man is deliberately
cruder, less acute, more forceful. His constant use of the word
"shit" apparently caused censorship problems when a possible
stage production of *Landscape* was being discussed, Pinter
being unwilling to part with it. Strangely enough for a Pinter play,
the woman is the more real, the more alive and sympathetic of
the two characters, and there is a good deal more compassion
than usual in the author's understanding of her. *Landscape* is a
not inconsiderable piece of writing, but it is a play of words rather
than theatre and probably ideally presented as a radio play. Two
speeches are enough to suggest the quality of the characters –
First, the man:

---

14. Since this book went to press, *Landscape* has been performed on the stage.
It was presented in a double bill with a later play, *Silence,* by the Royal
Shakespeare Company, at the Aldwych Theatre.

This beer is piss, he said. Undrinkable. There's nothing wrong with the beer, I said. Yes there is, he said, I just told you what was wrong with it. It's the best beer in the area, I said. No it isn't, this chap said, it's piss. The landlord picked up the mug and had a sip. Good beer, he said. Someone's made a mistake, this fellow said, someone's used this pintpot instead of the boghole.

Then the woman, some moments later:

I drew a face in the sand, then a body. The body of a woman. Then the body of a man, close to her, not touching. But they didn't look like anything. They didn't look like human figures. The sand kept on slipping, mixing the contours. I crept close to him and put my head on his arm, and closed my eyes. All those darting red and black flecks, under my eyelid. I moved my cheek on his skin. And all those darting red and black flecks, moving about under my eyelid. I buried my face in his side and shut the light out.

What *is* Harold Pinter's achievement as a dramatist? He has defined his position in the modern theatre with a disarming modesty that underrates considerably what he has accomplished – but which has also a grain of truth:

It's a great mistake to pay any attention to [the critics]. I think, you see, that this is an age of such overblown publicity and over-emphatic pinning down. I'm a very good example of a writer who can write, but I'm not as good as all that. I'm just a writer; and I think that I've been overblown tremendously because there's a dearth of really fine writing, and people tend to make too much of a meal. All you can do is try to write as well as you can.[15]

Pinter is the paradox of a thoroughly traditional playwright, a man with a keen sense of theatre, of carefully shaping a play into acts with strong curtains, and yet a writer so individual that the term "Pinteresque" has become part of the standard critical vocabulary. With the exception of *Landscape,* Pinter's plays have become gradually more and more traditional, culminating in *The Homecoming,* in which the only novelty is the occasional use of shock tactics in the language and behaviour of the characters. Most people would agree, even though they might hate *The Homecoming,* that it is superbly well done; the only question is, was it worth doing – or, less emphatically, is the play for all its skill

---

15. *Theatre at Work,* ed. Charles Marowitz and Simon Trussler (London: Methuen, 1967), p. 108.

of any stature, or simply a lively evening's entertainment? I have a suspicion that *The Homecoming* is finally a very thin play. One of the best essays to date on Pinter is Hugh Nelson's "*The Homecoming*: Kith and Kin",[16] a sensitive and very intelligent article relating Pinter to playwrights such as Ibsen, and *The Homecoming* to Shakespeare's *Troilus and Cressida* and the Biblical stories of the return of the prodigal and of Ruth. These suggestions of possible influences on Pinter's work are very convincing, though certainly they would seem to have been unconscious influence so far as Pinter was concerned. However, when one contrasts *The Homecoming* with the works from which it may have been drawn, the comparative lack of substance in the Pinter play is depressingly apparent. It is possible that Pinter has not as yet had in any of his plays anything particularly profound to say; that the verbal fireworks and mystery of the earlier plays helped partly to conceal this, as Christopher Fry's ornate language often disguised a similar lack; and that the increased discipline and clarity of *The Homecoming*, which make it in many ways a better play than its predecessors, at the same time reveal the comparative lack of depth and reverberation of what is being said. A very marked change of language has accompanied the growing discipline of Pinter's plays. By the time of *The Homecoming*, the exuberance of language has abated, the arias of strangely evocative nonsense have quite disappeared. Symptomatic of what has happened is what one might call the decline and fall of Pinter's legal jargon. In each of his full-length plays to date, Pinter has included a parody of legal or public-service jargon. Goldberg in *The Birthday Party* uses a soothing flow of civil-service phrases to pacify McCann, who is pressing him with questions as to whether this job will be like the previous jobs; Goldberg's words in fact say nothing, but McCann is reassured and satisfied. Mick uses a parody of legal terms to frighten and bewilder Davies in *The Caretaker*. In *The Homecoming* the parody has become a sudden, brief, but credible heightening of Ruth's language, reinforcing our impression of her as a hard-headed businesswoman, the language grotesque only because of the bizarre situation:

All aspects of the agreement and conditions of employment would

---

16. *Modern British Dramatists*, ed. John Russell Brown (Englewood Cliffs, N.J.: Prentice-Hall, 1968), pp. 145–63.

have to be clarified to our mutual satisfaction before we finalize the contract.

If the dialogue of *The Homecoming* errs, its weakness lies in being occasionally too forceful, so that one has the sensation of being hit over the head by the blunt instrument of its brutality. Quite unchanged is Pinter's ability to suggest character, vivid, larger than life, convincingly alive. Perhaps in the long run *The Homecoming* will prove not the least of Pinter's dramas in ability to survive in the theatre.

In a decade of many promising playwrights who do not manage to advance beyond promise, Harold Pinter stands out, for the originality of his vision of life and his use of language, for his sense of theatre, his general professionalism. He is simply better than anyone else around. To ask more of him than this is probably to demand what he has never thought of offering. To give him the last word:

> ... I certainly don't strive for universality – I've got enough to strive for just writing a bloody play![17]

---

17. Theatre at Work, p. 108.

select bibliography

PLAYS BY HAROLD PINTER

The Birthday Party and Other Plays. London: Methuen, 1960.
The Caretaker. London: Methuen, 1960.
A Slight Ache and Other Plays. London: Methuen, 1961.
The Collection and The Lover. London: Methuen, 1963. Revised
    edition, 1964.
The Homecoming. London: Methuen, 1965.
Landscape. N.p.: Emanuel Wax for Pendragon Press, 1968.

FILM SCRIPTS BY HAROLD PINTER

The Servant. 1963. Adapted from the novel by Robin Maugham.
The Pumpkin Eater. 1963. Adapted from the novel by Penelope
    Mortimer.
The Caretaker. 1964. From the play.
Accident. 1967. Adapted from the novel by Nicholas Mosley.
The Quiller Memorandum. 1966. Adapted from the novel by Elliston
    Trevor.

Later film scripts by Harold Pinter include *The Birthday Party*
    (1968) and *The Go-Between* (1969).

PINTER ON PINTER

"Harold Pinter" (interview with Lawrence M. Bensky, first published in the *Paris Review 1966*), *Theatre at Work*, ed. Charles Marowitz and Simon Trussler. London: Methuen, 1967.

"Harold Pinter Replies" (interview with Harry Thompson), *New Theatre Magazine*, II (1961), 8–10.

"Pinter Between the Lines", *Sunday Times* (4 March 1962), p. 25.

"Probing Pinter's Play" (interview with Henry Hewes), *Saturday Review*, L (8 April 1967), 57–97.

"Two People in a Room", *New Yorker*, XLIII, No. 1 (25 February 1967), 34–36.

"Writing for Myself", *Twentieth Century*, CLXIX (February 1961), 172–75.

CRITICISM

Amend, Victor E. "Harold Pinter – Some Credits and Debits", *Modern Drama* X (September 1967), 165–74.

Bernhard, F.J. "Beyond Realism: the Plays of Harold Pinter", *Modern Drama*, VIII (September 1965), 185–91.

Boulton, James T. "Harold Pinter: *The Caretaker* and Other Plays", *Modern Drama*, VI (September 1963), 131–40.

Brown, John Russell. "Dialogue in Pinter and Others", *Critical Quarterly*, VII, No. 3 (Autumn 1965), 225–43.

"Mr. Pinter's Shakespeare", *Critical Quarterly*, V, No. 3 (Autumn 1963), 251–65.

Burkman, Katherine, "Pinter's *A Slight Ache* as Ritual", *Modern Drama* XI (December 1968), 326–35.

Cohn, Ruby. "The World of Harold Pinter", *Tulane Drama Review*, VI (March 1962), 55–68.

Cook, David, and Brooks, Harold F. "Pinter's *The Caretaker*", *Komos*, I (June 1967), 62–69.

Davison, Peter. "Contemporary Drama and Popular Dramatic Forms", Kathleen Robinson lecture delivered at the University of Sydney, 6 November 1963. Published in *Aspects of Drama and the Theatre*. Sydney: Sydney University Press, 1965.

Esslin, Martin. "Godot and His Children", *Experimental Drama*, ed. William Armstrong. London: G. Bell, 1963.

The Theatre of the Absurd. London: Eyre and Spottiswoode, 1962.

Hall, Stuart. "Home, Sweet Home", *Encore,* XII (July-August 1965), 30–34.

Hinchliffe, Arnold P. "Mr. Pinter's Belinda", *Modern Drama,* XI (September 1968), 173–79.

Hoffer, Jacqueline. "Pinter and Whiting: Two Attitudes towards the Alienated Artist", *Modern Drama,* IV (1961–1962), 402–8.

Kerr, Walter. *Harold Pinter.* ("Columbia Essays on Modern Writers.") New York and London: Columbia University Press, 1967.

Leech, Clifford. "Two Romantics: Arnold Wesker and Harold Pinter", *Contemporary Theatre, Stratford-upon-Avon Studies 4.* London: Edward Arnold, 1962.

Mast, Gerald. "Pinter's Homecoming", *Drama Survey,* VI (Spring 1968), 266–77.

Morris, Kelly. "The Homecoming", *Tulane Drama Review,* XI (Winter 1966), 185–91.

Nelson, Hugh. "*The Homecoming*: Kith and Kin", *Modern British Dramatists,* ed. John Russell Brown. Englewood Cliffs, N.J.: Prentice-Hall, 1968.

Pesta, John. "Pinter's Usurpers", *Drama Survey,* VI (Spring–Summer 1967), 54–64.

Schechner, Richard. "Puzzling Pinter", *Tulane Drama Review,* XI (Winter 1966), 176–84.

Storch, R.F. "Harold Pinter's Happy Families", *Massachusetts Review,* VIII (Autumn 1967), 703–12.

Sykes, Alrene. "Harold Pinter's Dwarfs", *Komos,* I (June 1967), 70–75.

Introduction to *The Caretaker.* Sydney: Hicks Smith, 1965.

Taylor, J.R. *Anger and After.* London: Methuen, 1962.

Walker, Augusta. "Messages from Pinter", *Modern Drama,* X (May 1967), 1–10.

AUTHOR'S NOTE

Since this book went to press, Harold Pinter has published *Landscape* and *Silence* (London: Methuen, 1969) and *Poems* (Great Britain: Enitharmon Press, 1968).
Critical works which have appeared are:
Esslin, Martin. *Harold Pinter.* Hanover: Friedrich Verlag, 1967.

Gordon, Lois G. *Stratagems to Uncover Nakedness.* Columbia, Missouri:
    University of Missouri Press, 1969.
Hinchliffe, Arnold. *Harold Pinter.* N.Y.: Twayne Publishers, Inc.,
    1967.

index